Praise for
The Stone from Halfway Rock

"Anyone who has ever prowled through life filled with a sense of wonder and adventure will love reading Peter Blachly's latest book, *The Stone from Halfway Rock*. Written with spare elegance and a keen eye for dramatic detail, the first part of the narrative offers a fast-paced account of outrageous adventures Blachly and his siblings had on land and at sea during summers spent in a rustic home on remote Sheep Island in Maine. Time inevitably moves us away from the summertime rituals of our youth, and when Blachly returns to Sheep Island as an adult after a long hiatus, he offers a poignant (as well as practical) look at the ways family relationships—and the care and sharing of treasured family homesteads—can become more complicated over time. Filled with wonderful photographs that help tell the story, *The Stone from Halfway Rock* is a beautiful exploration of how our hearts and our most beloved landscapes become entwined, and a reminder that adventure awaits us every day if we remain open to it."

— WILLIAM F. WELD, former Governor of Massachusetts

Peter Blachly's *The Stone from Halfway Rock* reads like a modern-day *Robinson Crusoe*, but based on the real-life adventures of the longtime Maine resident and world-wide wanderer. In this polished, fast-moving memoir, Blachly writes about the early years he and his brothers spent on Sheep Island in Harpswell building fast boats, exploring the coast, and generally testing the patience and boundaries of their parents with their risky adventures. After following his sense of adventure around the globe, Blachly returned to Maine, reconnected with his family roots – and some of the beloved boats of his youth – and helped preserve the family cottage for future generations. *The Stone from Halfway Rock* is a deeply personal account of one man's connections to a specific, sacred place, but it's a universal tale because it represents the story of so many.

— BOB KEYES, Chairman of the Maine Arts Commission, author of *The Isolation Artist*

"Bath resident Peter Macdonald Blachly has written in *The Stone from Halfway Rock* an engaging, personal and nostalgic memoir of growing up on the Maine Coast in the mid-20th century. With his unerring eye for boats, tides, shoals and Maine characters, he paints a vivid picture of a more innocent era that is a delight to read. *The Stone from Halfway Rock* rightly joins the august canon of Maine literature and should be a valued addition to the book shelves of all Down Easters and those who love the Maine coast. Perfect reading for an afternoon on the porch overlooking the water."

— THOMAS E. CROCKER, author of *Captain Hale's Covenant*

"Luminous…lyrical…Peter Blachly's stories of childhood summers in Maine are a wondrous reminder of what's important in life. He has me laughing, weeping, visualizing seals and summer storms, remembering the smell of sea air, and promising myself to love the simple things."

— CHELLIS GLENDINNING, author of *My Name is Chellis* and *I'm in Recovery from Western Civilization.*

The Stone from Halfway Rock
Revisited

A Lifetime of Adventures on the Coast of Maine

Peter Macdonald Blachly

SHEEP ISLAND PRESS

The Stone from Halfway Rock Revisited—
A Lifetime of Adventures on the Coast of Maine

by Peter Macdonald Blachly

petermacdonaldblachly@gmail.com

© 2025 Peter Macdonald Blachly

www.petermacdonaldblachly.com

Published by Sheep Island Press

All rights reserved. No part of this book may be used or reproduced by any means without he written permission of the author except in the case of brief quotations embodied in critical articles and reviews.

Library of Congress Control Number: 2025903395

ISBN: 978-1-7372280-2-8 (paperback)

Book and Cover Design: Chris Molé, Book Savvy Studio

First Print Edition © 2016 Peter Macdonald Blachly
Second (expanded) Edition © 2025 Peter Macdonald Blachly

Printed in the United States of America

In Memory of

Elisabeth Macdonald Haughwout Blachly (1911 – 1973)

Frederick Johnson Oatman Blachly (1917 – 2016)

Frederick James Blachly (1941 – 2015)

Elisabeth Ann Blachly (1943 – 2015)

They all loved Maine and were instrumental in the author's lifetime of experiences here.

Special thanks to the author's wife, Johannah Harkness, whose encouragement and content editing has been invaluable for the creation of this book.

Contents

PREFACE ix
CHAPTER 1:   Piglet 1
CHAPTER 2:   My Childhood Vacation Home 15
CHAPTER 3:   Early Experiences 21
CHAPTER 4:   Charley Gomes' Boat House 37
CHAPTER 5:   Capsized! 47
CHAPTER 6:   The Butler's Cabin 53
CHAPTER 7:   Camping on Rogue Island 59
CHAPTER 8:   Betsy Boat 69
CHAPTER 9:   The Storm 77
CHAPTER 10:   Sherry Adams 85
CHAPTER 11:   Fire on Ragged Island 95
CHAPTER 12:   The Mystery of the Islands 103
CHAPTER 13:   Waterskiing in the Basin and Other Pranks ... 113
CHAPTER 14:   Uncle Clarence's Poetry
               and Other Summer Reading 117
CHAPTER 15:   The Hydroplane 127
CHAPTER 16:   *Sea Fever* 137
CHAPTER 17:   Return to Maine 147
CHAPTER 18:   Melody Enters Our Lives 155
CHAPTER 19:   Crossing in Fog 161
CHAPTER 20:   Passings 167
CHAPTER 21:   Home at Last & More Adventures 175

APPENDIX I: Creating a Lasting Legacy 193
APPENDIX II: Bylaws of the Blachly Maine
               Properties Association, Inc. 203

AUTHOR'S BIO 211

The Stone from Halfway Rock
PREFACE

When I was a young boy, I felt that I lived on the coast of Maine and merely spent the school year in Washington, DC. My love of the spruce forests, granite coast, fresh salt air, and the freedom of summer was so great that my nine months each year in a city 600 miles to the south seemed incidental by comparison.

My family's connection to the Maine coast began in the 1920s when my grandfather and some of his colleagues joined forces to buy a heavily wooded piece of land on the New Meadows River, about thirty miles north of Portland. They built log cabins, using trees from the building sites, and by the mid 1930s had created an idyllic summer community.

In 1956, when I was six years old, my parents bought a cottage on a small island one mile across the New Meadows River from my grandfather's place. Sheep Island had no electricity, no running water, no roads, no cars and no telephones. I felt it was the most wonderful place in the world.

My siblings and I quickly learned the ways of the forested islands and the ocean waters of Casco Bay. The lack of modern conveniences on our island added to a constant feeling of adventure. We carried water in buckets from a well located several hundred feet down a forest path. We got our mail, gas, kerosene, and some staples from Cundys Harbor, a half mile by boat to the south. We brought blocks of ice from the mainland every day or two to restock the ice chest. And in the evenings our light came from hurricane lanterns and Aladdin lamps fueled by kerosene. There was on Sheep

Island and the surrounding Maine waters a level of intimacy with nature that I have experienced nowhere else.

Our daily lives were heavily influenced by the beautiful but often raw and unforgiving weather. A pea-soup fog could blow in without warning and be dangerous, even deadly if one were caught on the water without a compass. The wind was generally mild and predictable in summer, but a strong breeze or storm could easily whip the waters of the New Meadows into a frenzy of churning waves unsafe for small boats. Occasional squalls and thunderstorms could be incredibly exciting, and equally dangerous.

Perhaps most importantly for me, life on our island required a degree of self-sufficiency, common sense, and patience—"tools for living" not taught in most schools, nor easily found in urban environments. If the outboard motor broke down we had to fix it, even if that meant taking it apart without a manual or a YouTube video to guide us. The mechanical and engineering problems of hauling a 1-1/2 ton dock out of the water required ingenuity and creative use of the materials and tools at hand. And if the rigging on the sailboat became tangled or broken there was no repair shop to take it to—we shinnied up the mast and fixed it ourselves, learning as we went how it worked. And that was how it was with everything: we learned as we went, extracting the most invaluable education from the demands placed on us by our rugged but beautiful environment.

To say that our experiences on the coast of Maine were formative would be an understatement. The emotional attachments that my family and friends formed for each other and for the area are so deep that many have moved here permanently, and the ones who haven't are drawn here year after year as if by a homing instinct, passing to their children and grandchildren their love of nature and the spiritual renewal that is the natural by-product of simple living. For my family, our little island on the coast of Maine has turned out to be one of the only places in America where we can still find freedom from the numbing bombardment of telephones, internet, television, cars, electrical appliances, corporate advertising, and the hard-edged fruits of the industrial world that have come to dominate the quality of life in America.

The following stories are a record of some of the more memorable of my experiences, not necessarily in chronological order.

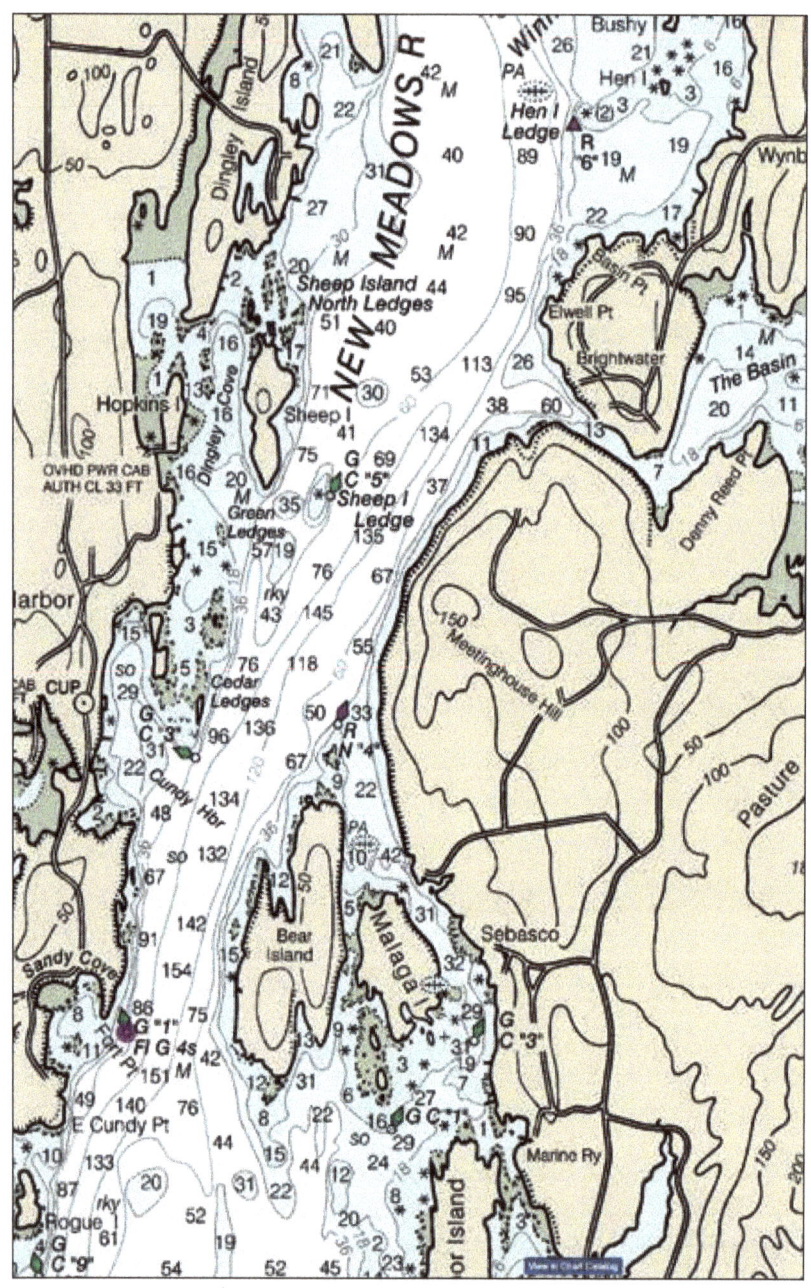

New Meadows River from Rogue Island to Brightwater.

CHAPTER 1:
Piglet

In the summer of 1960, I was ten years old. My older brother Sandy had finished building a small sailboat the previous year under the guidance of Charley Gomes, whose wooden lobster boats, skiffs, and sailboats at the time were widely considered the best and most beautiful on Casco Bay. Charley had suggested an unusual and experimental design for my brother's boat. It was ten feet long, a little over three feet wide, and flat-bottomed with a steel centerboard. Both stem and stern were squared off like a barge, and it was

"Sandy" sailing Piglet, 1959.

outfitted like an old-fashioned Friendship Sloop, with a bowsprit, jib, and gaff-rigged mainsail.

The result, which Sandy named *Piglet* after the character from "Winnie the Pooh," was as odd as its name. It was a stubby little craft, dangerously unstable in the water. An adult could easily tip it over just by standing on a gunwale. It was also hopelessly slow unless enough weight could be loaded at the stern to lift the square bow above the tops of oncoming waves. Furthermore, it leaked, and nothing we did, including fiber-glassing all the seams, would stop the water from seeping in. It was not long before Sandy came up with a ditty referring to *Piglet's* two-boy crew and its most notable shortcomings:

> "One for Captain and Sailor,
> The other for Ballast and Bailer."

A couple of years later I would inherit *Piglet* as my primary mode of transportation, but that summer there was no doubt who was Captain and who was Bailer.

On the morning of the 21st of June, Sandy and I found ourselves alone on Sheep Island, left behind as punishment to complete chores we had earlier neglected. The rest of the family, with a picnic lunch on board, sailed *Royal Tern*, our family's 21' sloop, out to Flag Island. It was a beautiful day for sailing, with a breeze coming up fresh from the northwest. I was disappointed and resentful at being left behind, but Sandy had other ideas. At his instigation we quickly finished our chores, packed sandwiches and a thermos of milk, and just before climbing aboard *Piglet*, scribbled off a note we left on the dining room table: "Dear Mom, we took *Piglet* and have gone out, out, out..."

We quickly raised the sails, lowered the centerboard, and cast off from our mooring in front of *Rocky Ledge*, then caught the northwest wind and sailed south along the shore of Sheep Island with our sails set in a broad reach. When we passed the southern point of the island the wind picked up and we flew past Cundys

Harbor, through the Bear Island Strait and out to the open waters of Casco Bay. Wind and tide were both in our direction, and before long we scooted between Flag Island and Long Ledge, a line of reefs where thousands of seagulls and cormorants congregate. We set our eyes past Mark Island to East Brown Cow, a lump of rock still low on the horizon, and thrilled to see it pass to our stern less than an hour later. Then the wind started to fade.

Before long we were completely becalmed. We were several miles from the nearest land, and as I looked about us at the empty sea *Piglet* suddenly seemed incredibly small. For the first time since leaving Sheep Island I felt vulnerable. It was totally quiet except for the creaking of the rigging, the loose flapping of the sails, and the occasional cry of a seagull. The noonday sun beat down on us, reflecting blindingly off the backs of the ocean swells. We stripped to our waists in the growing heat and waited for the wind, trusting from our limited experience that a northwest breeze in morning would be followed by a blow from the southwest in early afternoon. Despite the calm, our mood remained buoyant as we finished off the sandwiches and the thermos of milk, which we had been dragging in our wake to keep cool, and discussed plans for the rest of our sail.

I was for tacking over to Ragged Island, a mysterious place where Edna St. Vincent Millay had lived in solitude many years earlier. But Sandy, after a squinting examination of the horizon, pointed out the lighthouse on Halfway Rock eight miles further out to sea. It was barely visible: only a tiny spire emerging through the haze on the furthest southern horizon. The prospect was awesome, but the challenge of sailing *Piglet* half way to Portland on the open ocean was too much for Sandy to resist.

We kept looking to the south for signs of a breeze, but there was nothing—only the ghostly sails of a charter schooner far out to sea. This reminded Sandy of the local yarn about a mystery clipper ship that foretold death within the year for anyone who saw it. I kept looking to reassure myself that the schooner did not have the square-rigged sails of an old clipper ship. Eventually the color of the water out to sea changed to a deeper shade of blue as the wind, true to our expectation, came up from the south. Our confidence bolstered, we set the sails for the long tack to the west that would put us within reach of Halfway Rock.

The afternoon wore on as *Piglet* struggled against the on-coming wind and waves. We had the sails as close-hauled as possible, trying to point up into the wind enough to make our destination. But in the roughening sea, waves kept slapping against the square bow, jolting us to a near stop and making progress slow despite the strong wind. We fell considerably to the north of our destination and overshot it by a couple of miles, then doubled back on a southeast tack and finally pulled up in the lee of Halfway Rock. I was tired and sunburned, and my clothes were wet with salt-water spray, but I was happy and satisfied at our accomplishment and ready to go home. Sandy, however, insisted on going ashore.

Halfway Rock, located midway between Point Small and Cape Elizabeth, about 15 miles out to sea from Sheep Island.

There are very few things so terrifying as the look and sound of large swells gathering themselves up and crashing on a rocky shore far out to sea. Each wave rises like a prehistoric beast, then explodes into a burst of spray as it dashes itself upon the rocks. The sound is deep and dangerous and sends a primal shiver through the spine of any sailor, for it is the sound of shipwreck and doom. The prospect of landing an awkward ten-foot craft like *Piglet* in such conditions seemed foolhardy, even to me. I looked at Sandy with the gravest apprehension, examining his face for any sign that he might be teasing me. But he was serious. We sailed back and forth, riding up and down the swells, looking for a spot to land. There were none that looked safe to me, but Sandy settled on a little inlet between two boulders that appeared to end in a rocky beach.

Halfway Rock from the air looking northeast. The author and his brother landed Piglet in the cove at the top left of the island.

We lowered the sails and raised the centerboard. I paddled while Sandy steered. A swell rose up behind us, picked us up and hurled us, surfing towards the rocks. I was certain we would crash, but Sandy was skilled with the tiller. We whizzed between the boulders, spray breaking on both sides, and bumped to a sudden stop as the wave spent itself against the shore. We both jumped out, knee deep into the churning foam, our feet slipping on seaweed-covered rocks, and hauled *Piglet* up and out of reach of the waves and the incoming tide. Our exploration of the island would have to be brief, for we were already well into the mid-afternoon.

Halfway Rock was hardly more than a large reef, rising only about twenty feet above the sea. The only vegetation was a small patch of grass struggling against the wind at the top of the island. The place was dominated by the lighthouse and a marine railway that stretched a hundred feet or more to the water. At the top end of this railway was a Coast Guard dory, a double-ended rescue craft, covered in canvas. We had assumed the lighthouse would be manned, but no one appeared, and we concluded that it was deserted. The loneliness of the place was oppressive and there was little that interested us except thousands of ocean-rounded stones that lay strewn about the top of the island. Many of these were the size and shape of ostrich eggs and had been ground and polished to a near-glassy finish by the timeless action of the sea.

We were busy choosing a few of the most perfect examples as mementos when a Coast Guard sailor emerged from the door at the base of the lighthouse. We were surprised and a little nervous at the appearance of someone of authority. But we were quickly disarmed by the innocence of his tone and his extreme "Down East" drawl as he asked above the wind, "Where are you boys from?" Sandy answered that we lived on Sheep Island, near Cundys Harbor. "Where's that?" he asked. Sandy explained that it was on Harpswell, but seeing no sign of recognition on the sailor's face he simply pointed to the north.

The sailor turned and spent several seconds contemplating the thin dark line on the horizon. With a quizzical expression he looked at the sun, checked his watch, then asked in the same innocent tone, "Don't you boys think it's about time to be headin' home?" We agreed with him, quickly said good-bye and, stones in hand, started for *Piglet*. When we were out of earshot Sandy marveled, "He didn't even ask us how we got here!" In his tone there was contempt at the sailor's utter lack of curiosity and his failure to recognize the enormity of our feat in reaching Halfway Rock.

Landing *Piglet* had seemed to me an overwhelming challenge, but the prospect of getting back out against the surf appeared an impossible one. I looked at the waves, which seemed to tower over our heads as they crested and broke. Spray and foam blew off their tops, driven by the wind. The tide had risen considerably during our few minutes of exploration, and waves were already licking at the stern of our boat. We lifted the bow and swung it around to face the sea, edging *Piglet* forward until an incoming wave lifted it, forcing us back against the rocks. We struggled in the foam to hold our own against the force of the wave, and as it started to recede, carrying *Piglet* with it, we scrambled aboard, grabbed the paddle and a boat hook and did our best to avoid being dashed to pieces.

The surf was terrifying in a homemade 10' plywood boat.

Before we could clear the inlet, however, the next wave drove us back. *Piglet* bumped against invisible rocks and started to turn broadside to the surf, a position that would leave us helpless. Sandy lunged to the bow and pushed with the oar to keep *Piglet* facing outward. I tried to push with the boathook, but the rocks below were lost in seaweed and I kept missing or slipping from any surface I could find. As the wave receded, we were carried back out a little further, but we were still not clear of the rocks.

The next wave was huge. Sandy dug his oar into the foamy water to keep us moving forward. I threw down the boathook and paddled with my bare hands. The wave crested at our bow and started to break. Destruction waited only a few feet behind us. For a moment it seemed we were suspended at the curling crest with *Piglet's* bow hanging in the air. Then, just as the wave exploded into spray and foam, *Piglet* rode over the top and plunged down the back to safety.

We paddled furiously for several more seconds until out of danger. Then, riding gently on the swell, we looked back with relief, and basked in our achievement. I tried to memorize the visual details: the rocky, sea-weed-covered shore, the profile of the island with its lonely lighthouse and marine railway silhouetted against the sky, and the exploding spray as wave after wave crashed against the rocks. Sandy turned to me with a wry smile that spoke of pride and daring, as if we had pulled off a trick all at once on our parents, the Coast Guard, and the all-powerful sea. My admiration for my brother was redoubled, and I swelled with quiet satisfaction at being a part of this undertaking. We then raised sails and began the long trip home. Several rounded stones, proof of our adventure, rolled gently in the bilge.

As the afternoon wore on, we were overtaken by hunger and thirst, and growing anxiety that we might not make it back to our home waters of the New Meadows River before the wind died. But there were other things to fear. Our course led us through a scattered maze of reefs and rocks, many of which were visible only at the lowest tides. We had heard some of their peculiar names from our lobsterman friends: Bold Dick, Blacksnake Ledge, Round Rock, Holbrook's Ledge, the Sisters, Jenny Ledge, Dick Shoal, David Castle and many, many others, but we had never been out this far before. As we sailed through this gauntlet, most were visible, marked by

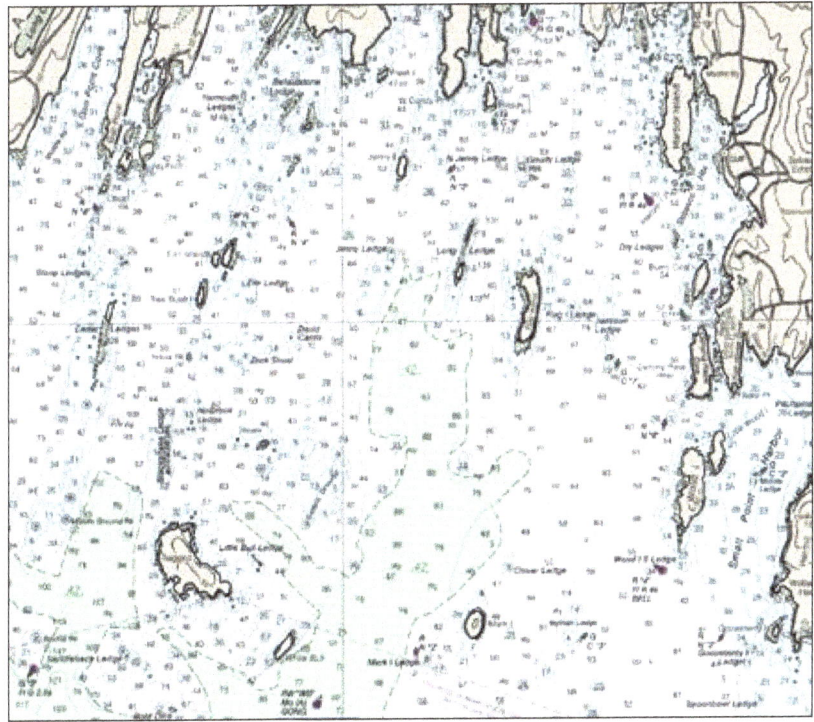

Casco Bay from Ragged Island to Rogue Island.

awesome explosions of white spray as the surf broke upon them. We gave them wide berth, for we suspected that where there was one, others might be lurking below the surface.

    Sailing with the wind astern, however, can have a lulling effect on a sailor. Instead of the brisk feeling of wind in one's face and of fighting the waves, the sensation is one of relative calm: the boat is gently pushed along, gliding up and down with the swells. The sun feels warmer, the afternoon sleepy. We had passed Ragged Island when we were alarmed to hear the brushing of kelp against the bottom of the boat. For a moment we were in a valley between two large swells. With the centerboard up *Piglet* drew only a few inches, but the tiller jolted in Sandy's hands as the rudder hit bottom. I looked over the side to see waving fronds of brown kelp, a sure sign that we were directly on top of a ledge. I turned to Sandy in terror. But the swell lifted and carried us past. The next wave swirled and broke on the reef just yards behind us. Sandy and I looked at each other saying nothing. We both knew how close we had come to losing *Piglet*.

I imagined the scene: shattered plywood and broken spars wallowing in the sea, two young boys struggling in the huge swells far from land. I renewed my lookout, and for some time suspected that under every whitecap was a deadly reef waiting to destroy us. I didn't relax until we reached the more familiar waters near Flag Island.

Just before sunset, between Flag and Bear Island, we were approached by *Loa Lea*, Dutch Albertson's big lobster boat that had rescued us when *Royal Tern* capsized four years earlier. Since then, he had taken my older brothers lobstering several times, and had always gone out of his way to be friendly and helpful. In the absence of our father, who was back in DC for most of the summer, Dutch was the person our mother was most likely to turn to in an emergency.

As *Loa Lea* pulled close we could see our mother on board. She looked distraught, and her voice had an accusing tone as she demanded, "Where have you *been*?" Sandy responded, "We've been to Halfway Rock!" Looking confused, she turned for a hasty consultation with Dutch, whose face betrayed a knowing smile. Dutch knew about boys, and he knew about the water. And we knew he was on our side. We watched Mom's face drop as he explained to her where Halfway Rock was. She turned and shouted even more accusingly, "The Coast Guard has been searching for you all afternoon!" We shrugged helplessly, and Sandy muttered under his breath that they must not have been looking very hard.

I had not imagined how my mother might have been feeling. She later told us that she thought that the scribbled letter we left on the dining room table was a suicide note. She thought the certain death of her two boys was her fault, that she had been too severe in excluding us from the family outing over so small an infraction as failing to make our beds right after breakfast. With no telephone, a pathetically slow skiff, with our father stuck at work in Washington, DC and unable to offer any support, she had spent the day in a state of extreme anxiety and guilt. But Sandy and I were too young and self-absorbed to feel any empathy or to think about her concerns.

Dutch offered us a tow, but we refused. Sandy was sure we could make it home despite the failing wind, and we were both attached to the idea of completing our epic journey under sail. Mom reluctantly agreed to our proposition and said that she would save some dinner for us. With a nod and a wave Dutch gunned the powerful Ford V8 and *Loa Lea* sped away with a roar.

As the sound of the big lobster boat faded in the distance, a dreamlike quiet flooded back on us, and for some time we sailed on in silence, watching the sunset. Gradually, the light faded, and the last remnants of breeze deserted us. Only the tide carried *Piglet* silently into the mouth of the Bear Island Strait. Soon we were enveloped in darkness. We could hear the ocean swells spending themselves against the rugged granite shore of the island. We could hear fish jumping near us, and porpoises snorting for air as they surfaced within feet of our boat. We could see the lights of Cundys Harbor and the cottages in the distance along the northern shores of the New Meadows. But in the murky darkness around us we measured our forward progress by watching the black treetops of Bear Island glide past the stars.

For another half hour we drifted along until the tide, which had reached its flood, started to turn against us. We resorted to paddling, taking turns with the oar. But our forward progress was slowed by the current. Then the mosquitoes found us. At first there were only a few, and we were able to dispatch them as they landed on us. But before long we were under full-scale attack, against which we were nearly helpless with our unprotected, sunburned arms, legs and faces. We could not fight the mosquitos while struggling against the tide, and we were quickly reduced to despair.

We called for help, yelling at the top of our lungs for our brother Jon. We stretched out the single syllable of his name in a hopeless attempt to make our voices carry more than a mile to Sheep Island. The only answer was the echo of our own voices off Bear Island and the further shore of Harpswell. For some time we struggled on, our pride and sense of accomplishment shattered.

Finally, in the distance we heard an outboard motor approaching and saw the beam of a flashlight swinging back and forth across

Dinner table on the porch at Rocky Ledge. Watercolor by the author.

the water. In a few moments our family skiff came along side. At Mom's insistence Jon had finally come to give us a tow. Still swatting at the armies of mosquitoes, we snatched for the tow line and begged him to hurry. The indignity of ending our great adventure under tow, breathing fumes behind an outboard motorboat, was a welcome alternative to the torment we had undergone for the past hour.

By 10:30 pm we were home on Sheep Island eating a reheated dinner and sharing the exciting elements of our sail. Even the misery of fighting mosquitoes was transformed into something noble in the re-telling. We tracked our journey on a chart of the Casco Bay and tried to identify by their unusual names the many ledges we had passed. Mom looked on with restrained tolerance, grateful that we were alive, but unsure if she should punish us for undertaking such a foolhardy and dangerous adventure. A fire crackled in the Franklin stove and the soft light of Aladdin lamps gave the cottage a cozy glow. Outside in the darkness, *Piglet* rode proudly at its mooring.

The Stone from Halfway Rock. Watercolor by the author.

Rocky Ledge in the early days.

CHAPTER 2:
My Childhood Vacation Home

I would like to take a moment and invite you to get a sense of what it is like at *"Rocky Ledge."* There is no running water here; no electricity, plumbing, and no telephones. Nor is there television, nor internet on this small island on the New Meadows River. The cottage has no insulation, no drywall, no plaster, no wiring. It is a frame structure of 2 x 3 studs and shiplap siding that was built in 1911 by Howard Goddard, a local lobsterman from the next island to the north. He used only hand tools, for back then there were no power tools, and certainly no way to bring electricity to this out-of-the-way island.

The room in which we are sitting serves as both living and dining area. It is an open space about 10 by 20 feet with dark wooden floors, weather-stained walls, and open rafters. It is quiet in a way that cannot be experienced in "civilization". We are barely 30 feet from high tide, situated on a small granite precipice overlooking the shore. Less than a mile across is the thickly forested shore of Phippsburg, largely unchanged for hundreds of years. Today there is an east wind blowing. But inside the cottage it is cozy, even without a fire. It is late afternoon and the only sound is the breeze whistling through the branches of red spruce that surround the sides and back of the house.

The dining area features a heavy oak table with thick, sculpted legs with lion's feet, surrounded by a number of antique wooden chairs. In the center of this table sits a kerosene lamp, our only source of light at the moment, other than that which filters in through the front windows. Against the far wall on either side of the south-facing window are two pieces of dark wooden furniture. On the right is a cabinet filled with dishes, tea cups, coffee mugs and glasses that have collected over the decades. And on the left is an antique dresser with a 4-foot-tall mirror framed in primitively carved wood. This piece of Victorian furniture serves as a catch-all. Its drawers are filled with board games and multiple decks of cards that have grown frayed and sticky from use, a box of poker chips, and note pads that have been used for keeping the scores of various games played on summer evenings. The marble top of this chest of drawers contains an array of oil lamps, including an Aladdin lamp with its tall chimney and gracefully-shaped, creamy-white shade. At night, if one sits close enough, this Aladdin can provide sufficient light by which to play cards or read a book.

On the north side of the room, adjacent to where we are sitting, there is a rocking chair and home-made wooden shelving containing dozens of books with faded covers and titles such as "The Fields of Home", "A Royal Tragedy", "We Bought an Island", "My Demon Motorboat", and a collection of books of poetry by an obscure American poet, Clarence Dan Blachly, my long-deceased great uncle. Also displayed proudly on this shelf is a two-foot-long model Friendship Sloop that was carved from a single log in the winter of 1958 by "Mr. Anderson," a lobsterman from Cundys Harbor, as a gift to my oldest brother, Jim, who worked with him as a stern man, hauling lobster traps by hand in the summer of 1957. Just behind me is a rusty Franklin stove, which on particularly cold evenings or mornings in June or September, provides enough heat to make the entire first floor of the cottage toasty warm and cozy.

The windows around us are simple affairs. There are six of them, all framed with calico curtains: four facing the river and one on each end of the room. The glass panes, dating from the first decade of the 20th Century, ripple and distort the images of the outside world, except for two that were broken years ago and replaced with modern glass. On the walls, wherever there is room for them, are

The screened porch, expanded in 1962, is one of the cottage's best features in good weather.

roughly framed paintings, pastels, and illustrations of sailing ships. And on the wall behind me next to the Franklin stove is a worn and discolored 1950s-era nautical chart of Casco Bay held in place by half-round moldings tacked around its edges. Through the front windows we see an expansive porch. It was renovated and enlarged in 1962 by a couple of lobstermen from Cundys Harbor who found part time work doing rough carpentry. The porch features 2 x 4 railings and large screened panels that can be taken down in the off-season. Much time is spent on this porch in the summer, for the views are extraordinary, and the older folks often sit for hours protected from mosquitos and flies, peacefully reading a book or watching the multitude of boats, both working lobstermen and pleasure craft, going up and down the river.

Imagine waking up in such a place to the fragrance of blueberry pancakes wafting up from the kitchen; coming down the stairs to see the early morning sun streaming through the front windows, casting long shadows on the table and floor and illuminating the steam rising from several plates of pancakes set out for the family. Imagine how, once breakfast is over and the most basic chores accomplished, we are completely free to do whatever may come to mind, whether it be swimming, sailing, rowing, driving the family skiff up to Cundys Harbor for an ice cream cone, going on longer adventures to nearby islands and beaches, or even exploring the Hester and Luther Little, two decaying four-masted schooners on the Wiscasset waterfront.

The author and his father climbed aboard the Luther Little (on the right) in 1961 and were able to explore her lower decks.

But first let me walk you through the rest of the house. The interior walls do not have studs. They are made of a single thickness of tongue and groove pine held in place by channels of quarter round moldings at the floor and ceiling. They rattle slightly if someone walks heavily from room to room. Moving to the back of the cottage we come to the kitchen, which is barely 8 feet square. There is a four-burner propane stove that must be lit by hand, but no refrigerator—only a World War One era ice chest sitting on the front porch. Drinking water must be brought over from the mainland in

5-gallon jugs. There is a catchment system for rainwater that can be used for washing dishes and taking sponge baths. Rainwater from the roof collects in a 500-gallon galvanized steel tank on a raised platform outside the kitchen window. A small pipe allows a gravity feed to a faucet above an enameled kitchen sink, which in turn drains out to a rock-lined pit, covered over by soil. Since 1911 this has provided adequate drainage for the tiny amount of water used for washing dishes. Early in the season, before rains have filled the tank, we must carry water from the island well.

In the corner of this small kitchen are a number of wooden shelves bearing essentials like measuring cups and other cooking implements. There is no empty wall space, for hung on hooks and nails on every surface are pots and pans, skillets and frying pans, measuring cups, muffin tins, and a primitive toaster rack that can be set on top of an open flame to provide a semblance of toast if one removes the bread before it catches fire. Two modern conveniences are found here: a fire extinguisher attached to the wall, and a Coleman Lantern hung on a retractable metal hook to provide light for cooking and cleaning up after dark. At the corner opposite the stove is the back door, which looks directly out on a forested hillside, at the top of which sits a simple outhouse. Just inside and to the left of the back door is a stairway, hidden behind a door that is constructed from the same tongue and groove lumber as the wall so it is almost invisible at first glance.

The stairs, barely two feet wide, ascend at a steep angle in the center of the house. At the top is a landing to the left of which is the "boys' room" extending some 20 ft from front to back. Two east-facing windows overlook the water and ensure that the first rays of sunlight will awaken whomever is sleeping here. On the other side of the stairwell is a nearly identical room where the grownups sleep. Just as in the downstairs, the outside walls have only exterior planking on exposed framing. The windows here also have rippled glass panes that distort the images from outside, much like the surface a pond that has been disturbed by a pebble.

The ceiling in both these upstairs rooms is simply the vaulted framing of the roof, with rafters set at two-foot centers supporting 1" pine planking of various dimensions. The affect is somewhat cathedral like, but austere and rustic in its simplicity. Nearly all the wood in this cottage is weathered, for in winter storms moisture from rain and snow has penetrated between the planks and left its mark. The beds up here have metal frames that have been painted white. There are no closets, but hooks on the wall where clothes can be hung, and a couple of dressers whose drawers stubbornly resist any effort to open or close them.

The walls here are also adorned with paintings and photographs by family members, as well as prints of square-rigged sailing ships making their way through stormy seas. The most notable feature is the overwhelming sense of quiet and solitude. It is peaceful in a way that can never be experienced in a city or town. There are no motorized vehicles, for the only way around the island is on narrow footpaths cut through the forest. Looking out the front windows from the upstairs bedrooms when the tide is high, we gaze down upon a granite shoreline with masses of seaweed extending out some 60 feet. Off to our right is a pier that reaches to the edge of the seaweed field, ending with a ramp to a dock that rises and falls with the tide.

Ours is not the only cottage on this island. As we go out the back door, the path to our left takes us to two others, and to the right another two cottages, all built in the first decade of the 20th century. Each cottage is hidden from its neighbor by thickets of pine, spruce, cedar and birch, and each has its own pier and dock. At the north end of the island is a compound of 3 more cottages owned by a single wealthy family—and continuing around to the western side is yet another house, a little more modern than the rest, built in the 1940s. Seven families in all, most of them having been here through at least two generations. We, of course, know our neighbors well, and we clearly agree that there is no more beautiful place, nor one more dear to us and our families, than this island and the cottages that adorn it.

CHAPTER 3:
Early Experiences

On August 16, 1956, just one day after his 81st birthday, my grandfather on my mother's side passed away at his family's ancestral home at Alexander Springs, just north of the tiny town of Belleville, Pennsylvania. I remember it well because our family was in Maine, renting a decrepit shack on Wynburg, a community adjacent to Brightwater in the town of Phippsburg. I will never forget the moment my parents drove away in our huge, black 1948 Buick Roadmaster sedan, which had transported our family of seven, plus two cats and a dog, from Washington, DC a week earlier. My four siblings and I were being left in the care of "Bunny" Berry, an attractive woman in her twenties and the niece of the woman from whom we were renting. But Bunny did not seem to know much about children.

As we watched my parents disappear around a bend, with oily exhaust from the Buick's tailpipe mixing with dust from the rutted dirt road, Bunny held my hand and asked me in a sympathetic, Kindergarten teacher's voice, as if she didn't know the answer, "Where are your mommy and daddy going?" My reaction, which surprised even me, was to burst into tears, exclaiming between sobs that they were going to Pennsylvania because my grandfather had just died. This was my first experience with death, and the sudden realization that my grandfather was gone from my life overwhelmed me. Bunny, who until that moment had thought I was a very mature and self-possessed little boy, was dismayed at my emotions and the torrent of tears her question had unleashed. I was inconsolable. She did her best, however, and eventually I was soothed by her kindness.

I do not remember much of the week that intervened before my parents returned, but memories of our rented shack are somewhat clearer. Even to my innocent and untutored eye, the place was little more than a dump. In earlier days it had probably been a chicken coop or tool shed. It featured three rooms, one of which served as my parents' bedroom. The others had to serve as entryway, kitchen, dining room, pantry and bedroom for my four older siblings and me. The was no plumbing or electricity, and I remember only screened openings for windows, though it is possible the windows were simply left open in the heat of August. The place was situated less than ten feet from the dirt road leading to Brightwater, and after a few days without rain, each passing car would stir up a cloud of dust that filtered through the screens and settled on everything inside.

The "bathroom" was a crudely constructed outhouse that was not even graced with a holder for the toilet paper. The inevitable result of five young children making use of free-range toilet paper was that many rolls ended up going down the hole into the murky and smelly depths below. After a few days and the loss of half a dozen rolls, my older brother Sandy, who was eleven at the time and already exhibiting a dark and sarcastic sense of humor, scrawled onto a piece of cardboard the words "Used Toilet Paper…Cheap", and tacked it to a tree at the edge of the road. This was before the age of indelible markers, and the lettering inscribed in pencil was illegible from more than two feet away. Nonetheless, my parents were less than amused when they returned from my grandfather's funeral, and quickly removed the sign. All of us children, however, thought it was brilliant, and, in my own impressionable mind, my brother Sandy became a hero, worthy of immeasurable esteem and imitation.

The shack on Wynburg belonged to Katherine Berry, also known affectionately as "Blueberry," one of the daughters of Dr. John Berry, whose father was a sea captain, Protestant minister, doctor, and one of the first settlers in the area. Dr. Berry was an important figure in the early days of my family's introduction to Brightwater. My paternal grandfather helped found the Brightwater community in 1925, and in the summer of 1927 began construction on the first of two log cabins. For temporary housing he built a pair of wooden platforms and erected a couple of surplus army tents, one for himself and my grandmother, the other for my father, age nine, and his seven-year-old brother, Howard.

One June night shortly after they had set up camp, a terrific storm came up. The temperature dropped while the wind and rain picked up, and before long the boy's tent was blown down. Drenched to the bone, my father and Howard retreated to their parents' tent, which was reinforced with a few wooden planks and

The author's grandparents and their two boys in 1927, the year they built Granite Ledge.

featured a lantern and a small kerosene heater. These 'improvements" did little good, for rain penetrated the canvas walls, soaking everything inside. As lightning flashed around them and thunder rattled the surrounding trees, the family sat shivering in the wet and cold. Suddenly, the front flap was pulled aside and a weathered and fearsome, white-bearded face appeared. "My name is Dr. John Berry," the apparition bellowed above the storm. "I am a medical doctor and I am ordering you to abandon this tent and join me in my house." Obediently, and immensely grateful, the family gathered a few things and trudged through the forest in the dark and mud to the Berry's spacious home a quarter mile away in Wynburg, where they were provided with warm baths, dry clothes, and civilized bedding.

Granite Ledge – built by the author's grandfather in 1927.

My grandfather's cabin, which sits high on a bluff overlooking the New Meadows River, was finished later that summer and dubbed "Granite Ledge".

Seven years later he and my father built a second cabin for Ms. Leora Field, my grandmother's best friend and former roommate at Oberlin College. "Aunt Leo," as we called her with great affection, was a spinster and social worker. Her cabin was a single room, though on a rather grand scale at 19 by 31 feet: the "golden rectangle" of the ancient Greeks, and the same proportions—though hardly the same dimensions—as the Parthenon. Our extended family now had two beautiful log cabins. However, neither of them was regularly available to us, for neither my grandfather nor Aunt Leo was willing to share space for weeks on end with such a large and unruly family. So, for the first few summers that I spent in Maine, our lodgings were mainly in Katherine Berry's shed.

The author's father, age 17, and grandfather in 1935, building the Field Cabin.

One of the features of life at Brightwater and Wynburg—a tradition that had started under the inspired guidance of Captain John Berry in the 1920's—was a Sunday night "hymn sing." In the early days there was a great focus on religion. In fact, the original inspiration for the creation of Brightwater was that it would serve as a summer retreat for YMCA staff and ministers in training. Although that ideal didn't quite manifest due to a shortage of funds from the YMCA and other religious organizations, most of the original families were deeply religious in their Protestant faith and attended the Sunday night hymn sings with greater devotion than—or perhaps as a substitute for—attending church.

As young children we looked forward to the hymn sings, partly because they would conclude with generous helpings of cookies and lemonade. The melodies and lyrics of the more popular hymns and songs worked their way into our memories and have remained there ever since. One of our favorites was "Steal Away to Jesus", which Sandy, much to my gleeful delight, corrupted to "Steal Away… to the Outhouse". There was no electricity on Brightwater in those days, and no phones or running water. My grandfather's cabin had started as a simple two room structure, but he added to it over the years: first a sleeping porch, then a second bedroom, and a sleeping loft over the "great" room. It even had what Sandy called an "inhouse", a composting latrine tucked away inside a closet in a corner of the entryway. We thought it was a really bad idea. The central room featured a massive fireplace and an impressive Estey pump organ with foot-operated bellows that clunked and wheezed when it was played. Oil lamps provided light after the sun went down.

One night the hymn sing took place at my grandfather's cabin. Many people had brought their own seating, for it was quite crowded. I was next to Sandy on the edge of a bunk bed at the back wall of the cabin. When song books were passed around I demurred, saying that I would just hum along—a comment that elicited much adoring laughter among the adults. I was embarrassed, for I could read neither lyrics nor music at age five, and I didn't understand why the adults thought it was so cute and funny. Nonetheless, I was reassured by the friendly reaction.

After 45 minutes of spirited singing, it was time for refreshments. Usually, the host family would bake something delicious, like chocolate chip cookies or carrot cake cut into cookie-sized squares. But my grandmother, a PhD political scientist and former Fellow at the Brookings Institution, felt that domestic work was beneath her. Instead of homemade treats, only store-bought Lorna Doone cookies were passed around, along with paper cups of Minute Maid apple juice. As Sandy helped himself to a handful of cookies he said, with a straight face, "Grandmother, you're such a good cook!" I thought it was hilarious, little realizing how offensive and demeaning his sarcasm was. Grandmother (who would not permit us to call her "Grandma") was gracious, ignored the comment, and quickly moved on with her tray of cookies.

Sandy's sense of humor was a wonder to me, though much of it carried a sharp edge of sarcasm that sometimes cut too painfully. It was not hard to see where it came from. My father, too, had a remarkable sense of humor and an extensive inventory of stories, puns, anecdotes, and off-color jokes that he could summon from memory at the slightest provocation. His lack of a filter, however, ensured that many of his quips were told at inappropriate times, or in the wrong company. The State Department, where he spent most of his career, was a breeding ground for such material, and he would sometimes come home and repeat at the dinner table the latest joke making the rounds at work, much to my mother's consternation and dismay. I learned a lot about anatomy from this unlikely source.

The origins of my father's sense of humor were harder to trace, for I don't remember my grandfather or grandmother ever making anyone laugh. They were both in their seventies by the time I arrived, and seemed quite serious and joyless. My grandfather suffered from cataracts and always wore a distinctive green visor to shade his sensitive eyes. It was not his only physical ailment. One day back in DC when I was too sick to go to kindergarten and my mother was too busy to take care of me at home, I was left in their care. Upon seeing my grandfather descending the stairs from the second floor, I greeted him enthusiastically. "Hello Grandpa, how are you?" He replied in a matter-of-fact tone that he wasn't feeling so good that morning because he was suffering from diarrhea—just the kind of news a little boy wants to hear from a white-haired old man! My matronly grandmother quickly settled me in bed and brought me a bowl with a slice of Wonder Bread soaked in warm milk, then left me to myself for the rest of the day.

Little did I know that my grandparents were actually amazing people. Both of them had Doctorate degrees in Political Science.

They had been Fellows together at the Brookings Institution long before I was born, and had authored many scholarly books together. Their 1926 tome on the political administration and economy of Germany became the blueprint twenty years later for much of the Marshall Plan and the rebuilding of German Democracy at the conclusion of World War II. Around the time of my birth they were in New Mexico, co-chairing what was dubbed the "Mini Hoover Commission", which rewrote the state's administrative structure.

My grandmother, who went by her professional name, Miriam Oatman, had been a Suffragette, organizing and marching for the women's vote. Her father was the famous hymn-writer, Johnson Oatman, Jr., author of "Higher Ground", "Count Your Blessings", and many other popular hymns that are still performed by gospel

Frederick Frank Blachly, Oberlin College 1911

Miriam Eulalie Oatman (Blachly), Oberlin College 1912

Johnson Oatman, Jr.

choirs all over the world. Miriam herself wrote more than 300 hymns and set some of her father's lyrics to music.

When she met my grandfather at Oberlin College in 1909, she was engaged to another man, but quickly ended that relationship. She and my grandfather both earned their doctorates at Columbia University before moving to Norman, Oklahoma in 1916 where my grandfather was hired as a professor, and where my father was born the following year. Miriam's documentation of my father's infancy and youth became the first published study of early child development.

She so self-identified as an intellectual, however, that when she suffered a mild stroke in 1962, rather than inflict her incapacity on her family or suffer the imagined indignity of mental impairment, she simply stopped eating, and died peacefully after 30 days.

My father picked me up at the bus station after school that day and delivered the news. His apparent lack of emotion about it was quite disconcerting to me. "Aren't you sad?" I asked him uncomfortably. "These things happen," he responded. "How was school today?" Something felt so wrong about this, but I knew nothing about psychology at the time and did not know how to put a name to it. Nonetheless, I was intuitively aware that there was something strange about my father's lack of emotion, so similar to what I had witnessed in both his parents.

In the final eight years of my father's life, as I took on the role of caretaker and advocate, he shared with me a number of stories about his parents and his own childhood. My understanding about my grandfather was further enhanced in 2020 when a long-lost manuscript of his memoir was found under a stairway in my Aunt's house. In partnership with my younger daughter, we transcribed, edited, then published *My First Life—Becoming a Man on the Colorado Frontier 1880—1905*.

Andrew Trew Blachly

My great grandfather, Andrew Trew Blachly, who struggled financially as part owner of the First Farmers and Merchants Bank of Delta Colorado, was shot and killed by bank robbers in 1893, leaving my grandfather, who had barely turned 13, responsible for providing for his mother and seven brothers. His memoir depicts a very hard life, but he managed to find some joy and amusement despite the hardships.

He was fond of writing limericks and using turns of phrase from the Bible in humorous ways. One rainy day in Maine as he and my father were walking down the hill between Wynburg and

Mary Adele "Dellie" Blachly, widow of Andrew Trew Blachly, with her eight boys, Thanksgiving Day 1893, two months after her husband's murder. Standing on the far left is Clarence Dan Blachly, age 12. Frederick Frank Blachly, age 13, is standing to the right of his mother with his hand on her shoulder.

Brightwater, he slipped on the mud and took a hard fall, breaking his leg. Despite his pain, he told my father with a wink that it was proof he was not a wicked man. Seeing my father's consternation, he explained, "In the Bible it says 'The wicked are made to stand in slippery places.' But I didn't stand," said my grandfather. "I fell down!" Later, with his leg wrapped in a cast for a couple of weeks, he complained to the doctor that it felt like he had ants crawling around inside. The doctor scoffed at such an idea, but my grandfather's irritation was so intense that the doctor cut off the cast only to find that indeed, a colony of ants had taken up residence there.

My grandfather's limericks were mostly written in the old style, where the last line is identical to the first, and they were quite tame. The raciest one he ever wrote, and the one my father loved the best and often repeated, broke with the old style and with his normal prudish restraint:

> *There once was a nun from Siberia*
> *Whose life grew drearier and drearier*
> *She threw off her habit*
> *And made like a rabbit*
> *And now she's a mother superior.*

But the most lasting tribute to my grandfather, by which most of my family knows him, are the two log cabins he built in Maine. He brought considerable experience to the task of building with logs, for his family's survival in the unforgiving winters on the western slope of the Colorado Rockies depended on creating shelters for animals and humans alike using only the materials at hand. In the late 1800s, he led his younger siblings working with logs harvested from the mountains to build fences, corrals, stables, a root cellar, and at least one cabin. That early construction and leadership experience helped put him through college working as a "straw boss", supervising a crew for the construction of the Oberlin Chapel. He also learned to work with dynamite, a skill he employed in blasting away some of the ledge upon which he built his first cabin at Brightwater, appropriately named "Granite Ledge."

During the summer of 1954, we stayed in Aunt Leo's "*Field Cabin*" for a week or two, and I had a chance to participate in a very small way in the construction of a kitchen addition. Until that time the cabin was a single room and did not even have a covered porch. The 10' x 10' addition, like the rest of the cabin, was built from trees cut on site, supported on the outer corners by slender columns of field stone and mortar. My principal job, it seemed, was to terrify my mother by climbing up and sitting on the roof while my father and older brothers applied shingles. I was just 4 at the time, and it is a wonder that my father allowed me up there at all, and that I didn't get hurt, especially considering that the ladder to the roof was a wobbly homemade affair.

I was not so lucky a day or two later when I accompanied my siblings down to the Wynburg cove for a swim off the community dock. I had not yet learned to swim, so while the rest of them splashed about, I played on the granite rocks between high tide and the grassy shore. Searing pain suddenly shook me out of my imaginary world. I screamed in agony and confusion, then started running up the hill, pursued by a swarm of very angry yellow jackets, whose nest I had disturbed. They continued to sting my arms,

The Blachly children in 1954 outside the Field Cabin (from top down): "Jamie" 13, "Betsy" 12, "Sandy" 10, family friends Margaret and Ann Bridgman, "Jock" 7, and the author 4.

legs, neck, and face as I raced along the Brightwater Road. I didn't stop running until I reached the steps of the *Field Cabin*, crying so pitifully that it took my mother a minute or two to figure out what had even happened to me. Luckily, I was not allergic, for I had well over twenty welts all over my body, to which my mother applied vinegar and baking soda. Fifteen minutes later I was back outdoors chasing after my siblings as if nothing had ever happened.

My mother became deeply enamored of Maine and was determined that her five children should be able to spend entire summers there rather than the two or three weeks allowed in those early years when we had to rent or borrow from a friend or relative. During the summer of 1956, after returning from her father's funeral in Pennsylvania, she found a deserted cottage on Sheep Island, across the river from Brightwater. It had been abandoned twenty years earlier during the height of the Great Depression and was so buried in overgrown trees that it was hardly visible from the water. A little research at the town of Harpswell revealed that the property taxes had fallen into arrears a decade earlier. My mother took a bold chance, borrowed $400 from our Uncle Clarence, paid the back taxes and moved us all in the following June. At any time for the next ten years the former owners could have come forward and reclaimed the place, but we were lucky in that regard and my mother's risky investment paid off in a huge way.

Our arrival in Maine in June 1957 was inauspicious. The trip from DC, which should have taken 11 or 12 hours, had taken about 18 due to a mechanical problem with our brand new 1956 Chevrolet station wagon, which replaced the 1948 Buick Roadmaster of previous years. The access to Sheep Island in those days was from Howard Goddard's dock on Dingley Island, about a quarter mile to the north of Sheep. Howard supplemented his lobstering income by renting parking spaces and dock access to several Sheep Island families, and by maintaining their skiffs in the off season. It was after midnight when we finally pulled in to Dingley Island. I was seven and barely awake, but I could sense the family's anxiety. It was pitch

Rocky Ledge in the early 1990s. Note the height of the surrounding forest.

black and there was a cold, thick fog hanging over the water. Sheep Island was invisible in the murky darkness to the south.

Our "skiff" was an unstable 11' rowboat, powered by a 3 hp Evinrude outboard—another new acquisition, and a significant improvement over a pair of oars. It took several trips for my father to ferry the family and luggage across through the fog. My mother and the two youngest boys—my brother, Jon, and I—were in the first group. Every surface of the boat was drenched in dew, and it was cold. With two adults, two children, and several suitcases, the boat was dangerously low in the water, and there was a labyrinth of reefs and mudflats to navigate between Dingley and Sheep. We inched along in the dark, my father dodging lobster buoys, and using the weak beam of a flashlight to stay within sight of the reefs without running into them, lest we be lost in the fog.

For the last hundred yards we were guided in by one of our new neighbors, Al Sargent, who kindly beckoned us over to his dock where we disembarked and unloaded our luggage. My father then headed back for another load of children and luggage while my mother guided her two sleepy little boys along a rutted path through the woods to our new summer home. The back door creaked as she pulled it open, and we were met with the musty odor from 20 years of abandonment. I don't remember much else. My mother somehow got us into bed upstairs where we fell instantly asleep. Eight hours later when we awoke, the fog had lifted and the sun was reflecting brightly on the water. Our adventures were about to begin.

Sunrise on the New Meadows. Watercolor by the author.

Charley Gomes in the living room of his home in Sebasco, 1960. Looking on is "Sheep Island Bruce", one of the Blachly family's collies.

CHAPTER 4:
Charley Gomes' Boat House

In 1957, when I first met Charley Gomes, I was seven years old. He was already an old man. His simple bearing belied his reputation as the finest wooden boat builder on Casco Bay. My mother had tracked him down the previous summer after falling in love with one of his sailboats, which we had rented for a few weeks in July. The boat, named *Arenjay*, was a green, eighteen-foot sloop with red trim, an open cockpit, and "Marconi" rig (a modern triangular mainsail). During the 1940s and 1950s Charley had built quite a few boats on the same lines. The design had become known locally as the *Small Point Class,* since most of them were owned by families living near Small Point, several miles southeast of Sheep Island. On weekend afternoons we would often see a whole flotilla of these beautiful boats racing on the ocean waters near Harbor Island.

I was only six the summer we rented *Arenjay,* and my education about sailing began the minute I stepped aboard. The boat was tied to the front of the dock at Wynburg, and our whole family was getting ready for a sail across the New Meadows. The sails were raised and flapping in the gusty wind when I climbed aboard. I ducked under the boom and stood on the far side of the cockpit, where, in all the commotion to get under way, no one seemed to notice me. I entertained myself by looking into the clear deep water over the side of the boat. Suddenly an offshore gust caught the mainsail and slammed the boom across the cockpit, hitting me on the shoulder and knocking me right out of the boat. By the time my oldest brother, Jim, had uttered a warning I was already thrashing around in the freezing water. I had not yet learned to swim.

Within a couple of seconds Jim and Sandy, who were 14 and 11 respectively, fished me out of the water and lifted me to the dock where I stood shivering while Sandy chided me for not knowing to keep my head down in a sailboat. The next day Sandy tricked me into learning how to swim by convincing me that a life cushion was supposed to be worn over my back instead of under my chest. After I had paddled around for a few minutes he confessed his trickery. I felt chagrined at being so easily deceived, but was elated that I now "knew how to swim."

At the end of the summer my mother sought out Charley Gomes and commissioned him to build us a boat *exactly* like *Arenjay*. During the winter she made several calls from Washington, DC to check on the boat's progress. He assured her that it would be ready for us when we arrived. Finally, in June, after getting settled in at Sheep Island, my parents loaded all the kids into the skiff and motored across the New Meadows River to check on our new sailboat in Sebasco. There were a number of boats moored in the cove in front of Charley's boat shed, but none of them resembled *Arenjay*. We tied the skiff and climbed up to peek through a window of the shed, but there was no sign of our new boat. My mother started to get edgy.

We walked up the road to Charley's house and found him just coming out the kitchen door, adjusting his tweed cap as we approached. Charley was a small, wiry man, slightly bent with age. His face was deeply lined, and his eyes had a mischievous twinkle when he spoke. He was wearing a khaki-colored shirt, and pants that bore traces of paint and glue. His hands looked huge, with broad fingertips and knotted knuckles. He greeted us respectfully. When my mother, masking her concern, asked him where our boat was he replied amiably that it was down in the cove, and suggested we walk down together to see it. I was too young to fully understand what was happening, but I could sense my mother's anxiety.

While we walked down the road to the cove Charley entertained us with a story about his recent trip to California. That winter he had married his housekeeper, some thirty years his junior, and had promised to take her in his brand-new Chevrolet sedan for a honeymoon to the West Coast. Charley had never been out of Maine and didn't trust his own sense of direction on land, so he had taken along a compass. Somewhere in Massachusetts he got confused at a traffic circle, and some time later happened to notice that his compass was pointing east instead of west. Still unsure of his direction despite the compass reading, and already disgusted with land travel, he vowed that if they ended up back in Boston he was going to give up and go home to Sebasco. Fortunately, he stopped for gas and directions just a few miles outside of Boston, and with the help of a station attendant was able to get back on the road in the right direction. Charley told us that he eventually got on

Royal Tern in 1960, after Charley Gomes added a bowsprit and larger jib.

Route 66 and made it all the way to the Pacific Ocean to celebrate his honeymoon in Malibu.

When we got to the pier Charley pointed to a beautiful white sailboat, floating like a swan in the middle of the cove. "There she is, Elisabeth," he said with obvious pride. My mother stood in silence for a moment. "But Charley," she responded, "That's not the boat I ordered."

Even I could see that the boat floating in front of us was very different from the one we had rented the previous summer. It wasn't green with red trim, but white with blue trim, and it was noticeably larger, both longer and wider. Charley turned to my mother and said, "Ma'am, I didn't build you the boat you ordered. I built you the boat you should *have*."

My mother was speechless. Charley took his skiff and towed the new boat back to the pier. Up close we could see even more differences: the cockpit was much larger than *Arenjay's*, and instead of a Marconi rig Charley had made our boat gaff-rigged, like the old fishing boats from Friendship Harbor.

My mother was so confused she didn't know what to say. The boat was beautiful, but nothing like what she was expecting. Charley explained that the extra length and beam, and the large cockpit would much more comfortably and safely accommodate our family of seven than *Arenjay's* narrow one. He also noted that a traditional gaff-rigged sail was much more to his liking for Casco Bay than a Marconi rig. It was useless to argue with his logic, and his gentle tone and absolute sincerity quickly disarmed my mother.

There were a few details on the boat to which Charley still had to attend to before we could sail it home. In those days, before the advent of high-tech fittings and fasteners, the leading edge of most gaff-rigged sails was held to the mast with a number of wooden hoops. Charley had made the rings himself from long, slender strips of spruce, which he first steamed then bent into 5" circles and fastened with copper rivets. A number of these were already encircling the mast, but Charley still had to lash them to the grommets along the leading edge of the mainsail, a job he did with remarkable speed as we watched in fascination.

He informed us that he also still needed to whittle half a dozen wooden rollers to ride on a piece of wire between the two ends of the boom crotch. This device kept the boom from pulling away from the mast, and the rollers allowed both the main and gaff booms to be raised or lowered without binding. Charley had brought in his pocket a number of small blocks of wood with holes pre-drilled in their centers. He started rounding off the corners with a chisel, but after creating five or six rollers he slipped and gave himself a very nasty cut on the middle finger of his left hand. Blood was going everywhere. I was taken aback, and my mother's voice betrayed a level of emotion that we all shared. But Charley was nonchalant. He calmly climbed up to his boat shed and came out a few minutes later with a big gauze bandage taped around the end of his finger. He reassured us that he was fine. "No boat of mine is complete until I've had spilled some blood on it," he said. He finished the last three rollers while his bandage gradually turned crimson.

I was deeply impressed by Charley during this first hour of our acquaintance. There was something incredibly appealing about his easy-going attitude and sense of humor, his skill with tools, his cleverness at finding solutions to mechanical problems, and his simple, unassuming manner. That *Royal Tern* was a product of both his artistry as a designer and his craftsmanship as a builder was not lost on me. Before we left he took us into his shed to show us some other boats he was building. He wanted us to see the basic components that had gone into building *Royal Tern,* from design to completion.

Charley Gomes' boatshed sat on top of a pier at the east end of the cove. Thickly set pilings, cut from whole trees and coated with creosote, were driven deep into the muddy bottom. They were joined and supported by lengths of rough-cut lumber, set at diagonals. Below the high tide mark the pilings were heavily encrusted with barnacles and green, mossy seaweed. At lower tides when one approached the pier in a small boat it had a dark and eerie feeling, like a decaying, ancient forest. The boatshed towered high overhead, and was accessible only by a couple of handmade ladders fastened between the pilings.

At the lowest tides much of the cove was nothing but a mudflat, so we had to time our arrival accordingly. At high tide the cove was transformed into a pleasant inlet. The pier was still several feet above the water, but climbing up was easy: the ladder rungs above high tide were free of barnacles and moss, and were worn smooth from years of use.

The deck of the pier and the sides of the boatshed were made from rough planking, weathered to a silvery gray from years of exposure to the raw weather of the Maine coast. There were a few spots where rotten or broken planks had been replaced with bright new ones, but these only punctuated the rustic feeling of the place. The pier was approached from land by a gravel road that had been oiled and driven on for so many years that it appeared to be paved. Among the bay bushes, oaks, and birch trees that grew along this road was a hundred years of boat-building litter: old, rusted marine engines and cast-off parts, a large bronze propeller, numerous rotted and broken spars, a rowboat with no bottom, a wooden keg full of rusty nails, a couple of 55-gallon oil drums, dented and disintegrating with rust. There was also the disembodied cabin of an old fishing boat. It was the kind of place a young boy couldn't resist.

Charley showed us into the shed, throwing open the barn doors at both ends to let in the light. The smell of sawdust, varnish, and glue permeated the air. The walls were hung with tools, lumber, wooden forms, shelves full of old paint cans and glue pots, models of boat hulls, barnacle-encrusted lobster buoys, coils of rope, and an aging calendar with an illustration of a five-masted clipper ship fighting heavy seas. In the center of the floor was the wooden skeleton of a new sailboat, and behind it the nearly completed hull of a "West Pointer," a large outboard skiff that Charley had designed. It was popular with local lobstermen for its stability, speed and smooth ride in rough water.

Half hull model of a Smallpoint Class sailboat by Charley Gomes. Photo courtesy of the Maine Maritime Museum.

Charley picked up a wooden model from his workbench and showed it to us. Carved out of solid wood it was just half of a hull, as if the model had been sliced from stem to stern straight through the middle. Charley explained that he carved models like this on a scale of one inch for every foot of the finished boat. When the half hull was shaped to his liking—he did everything by eye—he would cut it into sections every two or three inches and create full size wooden forms exactly replicating the shapes and proportions of the resulting cross-sections. Once the keel was laid and the bow and transom were in place, he would set these forms along the keel, turn it over, and build the hull up around them using 1" strips of pine, steamed, glued, and nailed in tiers all the way up to the gunwales. He would then strengthen the hull with oak ribs, chines and braces. Finally, he would add the floorboards and the planking of the deck.

As he explained the process and showed us the various steps on the new boats he was building, it all seemed very simple. Charley had only an eighth-grade education, had never studied marine architecture, and had no formal training in boat building. His methods were self-taught, and his designs were the product of his artistic eye. But all of his boats—sailboats, skiffs, and lobster boats alike—had exquisite lines; and whether standing at anchor or cutting through the sea they exuded a sense of grace, as if they were integral parts of nature.

I noticed that the transom of the West Pointer had a gap nearly

1" wide between the planks. I asked Charley about it. He explained that because the wind had been coming off-shore from the north, it had dried out and shrunk the wood, but that when it shifted to the south, bringing with it humidity from the sea, the planks would expand again and tighten right up. I found it fascinating that Charley had to take into account how much humidity was in the air as he put his boats together. Two years later, when Sandy was building *Piglet* under Charley's guidance, there was another boat-builder in Sebasco trying to imitate Charley's designs and techniques. Our loyalty to Charley made us resent the competitor, though Charley didn't seem to care. Our delight was unbounded when we heard that the first of these imitations sank to the bottom the night it was launched. We laughed and speculated, probably correctly, that the competitor hadn't taken humidity into account.

After we said good-bye to Charley, my parents took the four younger children in *Royal Tern* for the sail back to Sheep Island, followed by my oldest brother, Jim, in the skiff. As we sailed through Sebasco Harbor, my father, familiar with the channel since his childhood, pointed out the reefs and shoals while he maneuvered *Royal Tern* past them. He had learned to sail as a boy from Captain John Berry, and was fond of repeating Capt. Berry's first rule of sailing: "It's a good sailor who keeps a dry boat." My father explained that this meant always keeping the bilge bailed dry, but I later also took it to mean never pushing the boat so hard that water would come over the gunwales into the cockpit, threatening to swamp the boat.

As we glided along the shore of Malaga Island my father told us a little of the history of that troubled place [see "The Mystery of the Islands"]. Once we got out onto the New Meadows the southwest wind picked up and the boat heeled over for our first tack across the river. I sat in the cockpit looking up at the mainsail, enthralled by its graceful, upward curve. All the spars, as well as the oak combing around the cockpit, had a natural wood finish and glistened a rich, golden blonde under several coats of marine varnish. The sun-drenched sails shone a brilliant white against the cloudless blue sky.

On that first sail I studied every cleat, pulley, and line on *Royal Tern*. I was fascinated by the geometric layout of the deck planking, and by the gracefully curving shape of the tiller. I explored the spaces under the fore and aft decks, announcing to my parents that I could sleep there if we ever went camping. I made my father explain the use of every sheet and halyard—even the steel wire rigging. He went further, explaining the basic principles of sailing: how to keep the wind in the sails, how to "come about" (change direction against the wind), and what makes it possible to sail *into* the wind. My parents took turns at the helm, and even gave the kids a few minutes holding the tiller so we could feel the surging power of

Royal Tern under sail with the author's father at the helm, 1957.

the wind in the sails. The thrill was unimaginable, and by the time we reached our mooring at Sheep Island we were all deeply in love with *Royal Tern*. Charlie later confessed that she was his favorite boat, and the best sailboat he ever built.

CHAPTER 5:
Capsized!

A week after we picked up *Royal Tern* from Charlie Gomes my father had to leave Maine and return to Washington, DC. His two weeks of vacation each year were split equally between the beginning and end of the summer so that he could be on hand for the heavy work of opening and closing our cottage and getting the dock and boats in and out of the water. It was an arrangement that none of us liked—least of all my mother—for it left us fending for ourselves most of the summer. But it also forced us to learn and perform tasks that my father would have handled had he been there. The previous summer he had taught my mother and older siblings the rudiments of sailing in *Arenjay*. After he left, however, we were on our own to learn the finer points by trial and error. My mother was still a novice sailor, therefore, when she found herself alone as captain of the brand-new *Royal Tern*.

One Sunday afternoon on the first weekend in July, she took my brother Jon and me with her for a quick sail to see friends on Brightwater. It was a clear day, with a light breeze and an easy course straight across the river that did not even involve tacking—the kind of gentle sailing my mother liked, but which Jon and I found boring after the first five minutes. But by the time we headed home two hours later, with my sister's friend, Ann Bridgman, along for the sail, the weather had changed. As we left the cove at Brightwater we could see a heavy line of dark clouds to the west, and the south wind was fading. My mother eyed the clouds nervously and adjusted the main sheet. The clouds grew darker and loomed high.

We were sailing straight towards them, racing for home against the oncoming storm.

Halfway across the river the wind grew fickle, shifting aimlessly from South to West, then from East to North. The sky was now nearly obliterated by a boiling mass of black clouds. My mother's nervousness was tangible. Her voice quavered slightly as she gave us orders to trim the jib. Then the wind died completely. Our sails hung listless. My mother took in the slack on the main sheet and secured it to a cleat. The water was still. We looked around, confused by the quiet and the dark. Then, suddenly, a furious wind squall hit us broadside.

Royal Tern went right over. As I slid to the low side of the cockpit I watched with amazement as water came rushing in over the gunwale at my feet. It was a green, living thing, translucent like the top of a wave cresting before it breaks. I was mesmerized looking deep into that emerald green as the water poured in and filled the cockpit, swallowing our boat, swallowing me. For a moment I went under water. When I came up my mother was screaming at us to hold onto the boat, but her voice was nearly lost in the wind. *Royal Tern* wallowed on her side, nearly completely submerged. I pulled myself up and clung to one of the wire stays that held the mast in place. We were lined up along the gunwale, Jon in front, then me, Ann, and my mother at the back. The wind howled ever louder. Waves washed over the boat. Then the rain came, fiercely, like needles. Above the sounds of the storm came my mother's voice, begging us to hold on, trying to reassure us that everything would be O.K.

Strangely, I was not afraid. I took comfort from *Royal Tern*, embracing her wooden side and feeling confident that she was not going to sink beneath us. I marveled at how different she looked and felt from this angle. Her hull was smooth and white. I could feel beneath the paint the individual strips of wood that molded her shape and the change in texture where copper bottom paint met the water line. The sails were a wallowing mass of white, stretched out before me just under the surface. The rest of the boat was lost beneath the waves. Although I was shivering, it was more a thrill of excitement than from the cold.

Then, just as suddenly as it had begun, the wind and rain stopped. The sky was still dark above us, but the shore of Brightwater was awash in sunlight. Caught in the light of the sun to our east was a turquoise blue lobster boat, her bow rising high above the bone in her teeth as she sped to our rescue. Within a minute *Loa Lea* drew alongside. There were two lobstermen aboard, dressed in yellow rain gear. With their encouragement we swam over one at a time and were helped up over the steep sides and into the cockpit. We were safe! But *Royal Tern* lay wallowing on her side, nearly completely under water.

Dutch Albertson, at the helm, introduced himself and directed us to stand by the engine compartment where we could keep warm, while he and his stern man tried to figure out what to do with our boat. We were glad to comply, despite the powerful smell of lobster bait. But *Royal Tern* posed quite a problem. There was no way, apparently, that it could be righted, so our only option was to tow it back to Sheep Island as she was, mostly submerged, with sails and rigging sprawled out just below the surface. Even getting a towline attached posed a major problem: there was nothing strong enough to attach it to except the foot of the mast, which was three feet under water.

As we were contemplating this problem a couple of our neighbors appeared in a skiff. They had seen the whole drama from the front porch of our neighbor's cottage, where the five other families of Sheep Island had gathered for 4th of July cocktails. Al Sargeant and Phil Showell were both in buoyant moods as they arrived to help, and Al cheerfully solved our towline problem by jumping, fully clothed, into the ice-cold New Meadows River and securing the line to the base of the mast.

It took only about ten minutes to drag *Royal Tern* into the cove at Sheep Island. We were greeted by a flotilla of skiffs and rowboats manned by all our other neighbors. Everyone was congratulatory on our safety. But no one could figure out how to get the boat righted and floating again. The solution to the righting problem was soon analyzed: the weight of the water-soaked sails was counteracting the boat's natural inclination to right itself with 600 pounds of iron ballast at the bottom of the keel. Somehow we would have to lower the sails. Among our well-fortified and good-natured neighbors there was no shortage of volunteers to perform this aquatic maneuver. One after another jumped into the water to help. Within minutes the sails were down, and *Royal Tern* slowly rolled upright. Everyone cheered.

But the boat was still mostly submerged. The decks were awash, the gunwales underwater, and there was no way to bail her out or get her floating. Al Sargent solved this problem, too. At low tide his dock would be in less than three feet of water. Since the *Royal Tern* drew slightly more than three feet, all we had to do was tie her to his dock and wait for the tide to go out. Everyone cheered again. Dutch Albertson, confident that we and our neighbors could handle the problem from here on, graciously accepted our thanks while refusing the many offers of cocktails, though his helper looked disappointed, and went back to hauling traps.

Two hours later, as the sun was going down and the tide was reaching its ebb, we all reassembled in dry clothes at Al Sargent's dock. His plan had worked perfectly, and after 20 minutes of intensive bailing *Royal Tern* was floating again. We were all amazed to find under the forward deck a bouquet of flowers still intact, and a head of cabbage from a friend's garden on Brightwater. The anchor, oars, boathook, extra lines—all were there. The only thing missing was a small wooden bilge cover that had floated away on the tide.

The next day we sailed up to Sebasco to visit with Charley Gomes. My mother was no longer confident in the safety of her new boat, and wanted his advice and assistance. Charley reassured her that *Royal Tern* was indeed a good, safe boat. He put a few large pieces of Styrofoam under the front and rear decks so that if it ever capsized again we would not have a problem with floatation. As we were saying good-bye he turned to my mother and said good-naturedly, "Elisabeth. Around here we say that when the big black clouds come, it's time to take in the wash."

Moonlight on New Meadows. Watercolor sketch by the author.

CHAPTER 6:
The Butler's Cabin

During the summer, darkness comes late on the New Meadows. Well after the sun goes down behind Sheep Island the evening light still lingers over the water, and on clear evenings when the wind is still and the tide is high, the river takes on an especially magical aspect. On such evenings my brother Jon and I would sometimes sleep outside on the screened porch of *Rocky Ledge*. There we could watch the stars slowly appear above Phippsburg on the far shore and listen to the water lapping at the granite ledge below us. Sometimes we would also witness the rising of the moon and watch in fascination as its silvery reflection danced before us on the face of the river.

One night Jon and I were on the porch unable to sleep because Mom, Sandy, Betsy, and her friend Robin, were playing cards inside. Jon and I were the "little boys," and until our teens we were usually sent to bed earlier than our siblings. During the summers, in the tight confines of our cottage, this was an especially difficult policy to enforce, and we rarely fell asleep until the whole family was in bed, lights out, and conversations ceased.

Tonight, our perennial bedtime restlessness proved fortuitous, for no one inside *Rocky Ledge* saw the strange shimmering glow, which at first we thought was the rising of the full moon. For a few moments we watched as it grew brighter and took on a reddish hue. The light seemed to reflect in the broken clouds over Brightwater, but its source seemed unusually low in the sky, as if it were in the trees instead of above them. It was such an unusual spectacle that we called to those inside to come see it.

Sandy, who had gone upstairs only moments earlier looked through the bedroom window and yelled with alarm that it wasn't the moon—it was a fire! Instantly, the cottage was in an uproar. Footsteps thundered on the stairs. Dresser drawers and closet doors were opened and slammed shut. Instructions were shouted, and before Jon and I could get in a word about going along, Sandy, Betsy, and Robin had dashed out of the house, piled into the skiff, and started across the river.

In those days we had only a 3-horsepower outboard that pushed the heavy, flat-bottomed skiff along only marginally faster than it could be rowed. Mom, Jon, and I sat on the porch and listened as the boat crossed slowly to Brightwater. It was an incredibly still night, and we could hear the motor easily, even when they got to the other side. There was no dock on that part of Brightwater, so Sandy and the girls had to land on the rocky shore. When the motor was off we could hear the crackling of the fire and the sound of their anxious voices as they investigated the scene. Then we heard Sandy yelling, "FIRE!! FIRE AT THE BUTLER'S!" He was making his way around the Brightwater "Boulevard" to the north of the peninsula. Over on Sheep Island, we thought he was raising the alarm at each cabin, since there were no telephones on Brightwater. But something very different was going on.

Sandy, Betsy, and Robin had found the Butler's log cabin consumed by flames, but no sign of the Butlers. Leaving Betsy and Robin to make sure the fire didn't spread to the trees, Sandy ran along the road through the dense woods to the next cabin, but found that one deserted as well. Alarmed at this mystery he continued down the Brightwater Boulevard. By now, complete darkness had settled on the river. In the deep woods of Brightwater Sandy could see almost nothing at all. He was feeling his way along the heavily rutted dirt road. More than once he found himself amidst the trees at the side of the road. He tried to check his progress by looking for bits of clear sky between the branches overhead, but it was uncertain and slow going. Then he saw the headlights of a car coming in his direction.

It was Sunday evening, and all the residents of Brightwater had gathered at the Ewing cabin for the regular weekly "Hymn Sing." The car now approaching was returning early. Sandy flagged it down and hastily informed the occupants that the Butler's cabin was on fire, not realizing in the dark whom he was addressing. Jane Butler caught her breath and stammered, "Oh my God, the DOGS!"

George Butler told Sandy that everyone else was still at the Ewing's. He asked him to go spread the word, and to make sure the Phippsburg fire station was called. The Butlers then raced off to the fire and Sandy continued alone in the dark to the Ewing cabin. As he approached the door he could hear voices singing, "Pull for the shore, Sailor, Pull for the shore..." He ran up the stairs and burst through the front door with such energy and urgency that everyone in the room stopped singing and stared at him in alarm. "FIRE!" Sandy blurted out, "FIRE AT THE BUTLER'S!"

Sandy could not have been bearing more disturbing news. Everyone's immediate concern was for the Butlers, but the very real prospect of a forest fire added more urgency to the situation. Just twenty years earlier a fire had started on Elwell Point and had cut a large swath through the forest, barely missing some of the cabins. Jerome Davis, one of Brightwater's founders, immediately took charge, ordering everyone to gather buckets, Indian pumps, and any thing else that could be used to fight the fire, and to meet at the Butler cabin for a bucket brigade. He then drove, with Sandy in tow, to John Holton's house in Wynburg, site of the nearest telephone, to call the fire department.

The volunteer fireman who answered was not familiar with Brightwater. Jerome gave directions as far as the Wynburg road and told him that someone would meet them and lead the way to the Butler's cabin. Sandy reluctantly volunteered for this duty so that Jerome could get back to direct the bucket brigade. For the next ten minutes Sandy swatted mosquitoes while he waited on the road with Jerome's flashlight and listened for the approaching siren. As the fire engine lumbered along on the rutted dirt road, Sandy flagged it down, jumped onto the running board by the driver's door, and led the way around Brightwater's "Boulevard". When they reached the Butler's driveway the firemen found it too narrow to accommodate the fire engine. Sandy helped them unload and carry equipment by hand down the long dirt drive. It was heavy work for a 13-year-old boy.

By the time the Fire Department arrived at the scene of the blaze, there was almost nothing left of the cabin. The roof was gone and the walls had caved in, reducing the site to little more than a giant bonfire. The bucket brigade had been a total failure, for the heat was so intense that no one could get close enough to do any good, and the volume of water making its way from hand to hand up the rocks from the shore was so minimal that the effort was little more than symbolic. Long before the firefighters arrived the neighbors had given up on the cabin and were concentrating instead on the trees and underbrush around the edge of the clearing.

The volunteer firemen set up a gasoline-powered pump by the water's edge and were able to direct a remarkably powerful stream of salt water onto the blaze, sending up giant clouds of steam. The creosote-soaked logs and bone-dry timbers of the small cabin were burning so voraciously that even with this rig it took more than half an hour to control the flames. After the firefighters were satisfied that the cabin was no longer a threat—there was nothing left standing except the chimney—they directed their hoses onto the trees, many of which had been badly scorched or were already smoldering despite the efforts of the bucket brigade. If there had been any wind at all, the flames, which at times towered as high as a hundred feet, could easily have ignited the woods of Brightwater, or the untamed and overgrown forest on the opposite side of the Narrows.

By this time, a couple dozen boats had gathered in the Narrows in front of the Butler's cabin. People had come from Sheep Island, Dingley Island, Cundys Harbor, Birch Point, Brighams Cove, and other points around the New Meadows to watch the spectacular blaze and offer their help. Some of the smaller boats were able to land and were tied to the rocks. Larger ones jostled for position against the strong current. Several dropped anchor or had tied up to lobster buoys, while others continued moving about for the best view, or just to keep from drifting away. My mother, Jon, and I were among this Armada aboard *Little Effort*, a turn-of-the-century motor launch belonging to Al Sargent, our neighbor on Sheep Island. As boats continued to arrive, questions and answers were relayed back and forth: "Whose cabin was it? Was anyone hurt? How did it start? We heard that nobody was home..."

But the news that most captivated the imagination of the onlookers was that the Butler's two Irish Setters had been inside the cabin and were lost in the blaze. The Butlers had no children and were deeply attached to their beautiful dogs. Jane Butler was heartbroken when she arrived to see the nose and paws of one of her dogs protruding from the space under the back door where it had died while trying to escape. There was nothing she or her husband could do, and within a few minutes the walls caved in burying both dogs inside.

Word also got out that Jane Butler had left a diamond ring hanging on a nail in her bedroom. This information stimulated a treasure hunt in the days following the fire. At first it was just the Butlers' friends who poked through the ashes. But after they abandoned their efforts others moved in, and for the rest of the summer the site was a magnet for the young and the curious. No one ever found the ring.

After the flames had been subdued and darkness returned to the Narrows, most of the crowd started leaving for home. The Brightwater people drifted back through the woods, lighting their way with flashlights and lanterns. On the water, engines were started and boats motored away up or down the river. The Sheep Island contingent aboard *Little Effort* did not stay long. As we made our way across the New Meadows, Jon and I sat at the stern and watched the phosphorescence glowing in our wake. We were so tired by the time we reached the Sargent's dock that we could barely walk, and collapsed gratefully into our beds the second we got home.

Sandy, Betsy, and Robin were the last to leave the scene of the fire. They stayed until the firefighters had loaded up their equipment; until the Butlers, distraught over the loss of their dogs, had driven away, back to their home in Vermont; until Jerome Davis had inspected the site to his own satisfaction and gone home, taking with him a bucket left by a next-door-neighbor. When the site was completely empty, and all that remained was the blackened stone chimney and the acrid smell of wet ashes, Sandy, Betsy, and Robin got back into the skiff and headed home to Sheep Island.

CHAPTER 7:
Camping on Rogue Island

One bright day in July 1960 Sandy convinced Mom to let us take *Piglet* for an overnight camping trip. It took some doing, as the memory of our perilous adventure to Halfway Rock was still fresh in her mind, but she relented upon Sandy's promise that we would never be far from land. Our intended destination was Sandy Cove, a protected inlet on East Cundys Point at the southern end of the Bear Island Strait where we could haul *Piglet* safely up the beach and camp comfortably on the soft sand. About three o'clock in the afternoon we made our preparations. We wrapped our sleeping bags in plastic and stowed them under the forward deck where they were least likely to get wet. We made up a batch of pancake batter and poured it into a mason jar, filled an old jam bottle with maple syrup, and packed a stick of butter, forks, napkins and paper plates into a small cooler chest. We also brought along a frying pan, and Sandy managed to sneak into our supplies an old, half-gallon can of Maxwell House coffee with a few coffee grounds left in it.

The wind was from the southwest, and the sky was delightfully clear. It looked as if we were in for an idyllic sail towards the sea, and we were anxious to be under way. We were still proud of *Piglet's* accomplishment in getting us out to Halfway Rock and most of the way back just a few weeks earlier. After hasty good-byes we raised the sails and cast off from the dock for our first tack across the New Meadows. We sat as far back in the stern as possible to keep the bow above the tops of the waves, but the extra weight of our camping gear under the forward deck counteracted our efforts, and *Piglet* plowed squarely into every wave. As usual, I had to bail every few minutes in a vain attempt to keep the bilge dry.

Piglet's square bow made for difficult sailing in any kind of a sea.

Our spirits remained high, however, with the exhilaration of freedom: we had no set bedtime, no chores, and no one to answer to for the next 24 hours. But by the third tack when we reached the shore of Phippsburg on the far side of the New Meadows for the second time we were painfully aware that something was wrong. We were several hundred yards upriver of where we should have been. The problem was the incoming tide, compounded by the snail's pace of *Piglet* and the fact that it could only point up about 60 degrees into the wind. Sandy explained to me, with a great deal of aggravation and the first hint of condescension towards *Piglet*, that a *normal* sailboat can point up as little as 30 degrees into the wind. With both the wind and tide working against us in our already handicapped state we had little hope of making a quick trip out to Sandy Cove.

Tides and current on the New Meadows vary greatly during the course of each month. During "spring tides" when there is a new moon or a full moon and the gravitational pull from both sun and moon are combined at their strongest, the rise and fall of the tide can exceed 13'. But in "neap tides" between these extremes, when there is a half-moon and the gravitational forces of sun and moon counteract each other, there can be as little as a 6-1/2' difference between low and high tide. The strength of the current varies accordingly, with twice as much water rushing in and out of the New Meadows during spring tides.

Sandy, noting that the current was stronger in the middle of the New Meadows, resorted to a series of short tacks that never let us get more than a few hundred feet from the shore of Phippsburg. For some time we amused ourselves by playing "chicken" with the rocks as we approached the shore. We had our timing perfected. Thirty feet from shore Sandy would say "Ready about!" I would lean over and loosen the jib sheet from its cleat on the lee gunwale, the side of the boat furthest from the wind. Then, just as we were about to run onto the rocks, Sandy would say, "Hard-a-lee!" and push the tiller as hard as he could. As *Piglet* turned into the wind, I would let go of the jib sheet, and for a second the whole world would be nothing but flapping sails. As the bow continued around we shifted to the other side of the boat. I would pull on the other jib sheet and secure it just as the sails were filling with wind. The whole maneuver took about 3 seconds. We would then look back and check our wake to see how close we had actually come to crashing. More than once, just as we were coming around, the centerboard scraped against the rocks. We thought it was great fun.

Nonetheless, we continued to be disappointed at our forward progress. After an hour of making short tacks our patience was wearing thin. When we hit the current coming through the Sebasco channel between Phippsburg and Bear Island we decided to tack across towards Cundys Harbor. Our progress there was just as laborious, and we were grateful, after several short tacks, to sail into the harbor where the incoming tide had no effect on us. Once we got into the protected waters of the harbor, however, there was no wind at all. We had to paddle in order to reach the dock in front of Holbrook's General Store at the southern-most end of the harbor.

It was always a treat to go to "Christine's," as Holbrook's Store was generally known. Christine Miller, the owner of the store and

Christine Miller, beloved postmistress of Cundy's Harbor, behind the counter at Holbrook's Store.

postmistress of Cundys Harbor, was always kind and cheerful. She was about the same age as my mother. But her hair was graying and her face was so weathered from the Maine winters that it was hard to tell how old she really was. "Hello Peter," she would drawl in a thick local accent when I came in for the mail. She didn't say much, or ask much, but Christine had an air about her that made us think she knew a lot more about what was going on than it appeared.

Sandy and I tied *Piglet* to the dock, raced up the ramp and pier, climbed the graveled walkway past the rusting, hand-cranked kerosene pump at the corner of the store, and went in through the swinging screen door. Christine was about to close for the evening. "Hello Sandy, hello Peter. Can I get you boys anything?" We were already scouring the shelves for marshmallows and potato chips. "We're going camping," we told her as we fished for sodas in the ancient ice-chest at the back of the store.

Holbrook's General Store was small and had the feel of an old barn, with dusty windows, white-painted wooden walls, and plain hardwood flooring that had never been painted or finished. It was gray with age, and some of the planks bowed up slightly on the edges and felt funny under our bare feet. Merchandise was displayed on a hodge-podge of shelving: Hostess Twinkies, Wonder Bread, and other unhealthy baked goods on a wire rack in the center of the store; fishing lures and drop lines smelling of creosote on wooden shelves against the far wall, and cans of copper-bottom paint along the floor, along with several pairs of thigh-high rubber boots that lobstermen wore.

At the back of the store there were a few cans of household cleanser, Crisco, bottles of Karo syrup, and an old dairy cooler with a stuck door. The counter featured several big jars of assorted candy and a rack of postcards that depicted quaint harbor scenes like lobstermen holding giant lobsters, stacks of lobster traps next to fishing sheds on spindly piers, and lobster boats at their moorings. High on the wall behind the counter was a clock advertising "Miller Time", though Cundys Harbor was "dry", and a brightly colored, bas-relief logo of "Moxie," that soft drink peculiar to New England.

Christine asked us where we were going for our camping trip and nodded her approval at our answer. "Have a good time," she told us, "And watch out for the poison ivy." We thanked her and headed back to the dock, the broad planks of the pier rattling loosely as we ran across them. The smell of lobster bait and creosote hung in the air. Mr. Anderson's lobster boat, the *Ada* (named for his wife), was at the adjacent pier taking on bait. Old and weathered as granite, Mr. Anderson stood in the cockpit guiding a barrel being lowered to him by a hand-cranked winch from the deck twenty feet above. When he got the bait safely on board he looked up and greeted us, "Hello boys." His accent was so thick that "boys" came out in two syllables.

My oldest brother, Jim, had gone lobstering with Mr. Anderson several times a few summers before and his hard work had won the old man's respect and gratitude. The next summer Mr. Anderson presented Jim with a large model of a Friendship Sloop that he had carved from a two-foot pine log. The boat was complete with "wine-glass" hull, weighted keel, bowsprit, working sails, rigging and rudder. It was roughly but carefully detailed with a cabin, miniature anchors, and hatch covers, and it had a striking red and white paint job. Best of all: it sailed beautifully. However, out of a kind of reverence, we rarely sailed it, but kept it displayed in a place of honor on a shelf at *Rocky Ledge*.

Sandy and I returned Mr. Anderson's greeting and clambered aboard *Piglet*, cast off, and paddled away from the dock, not even bothering to raise the sails in the calm of the harbor. The wind was still blowing gently from the south when we reached the point. But it was mid-tide and the current in the Bear Island Strait was ominously strong. We resorted again to short tacks close to shore but were able to make almost no forward progress. After several tacks we had progressed only a few feet along the shore.

We gave up on sailing through the strait and tried paddling instead, staying close to the shore. Since we had only one oar Sandy did the paddling while I steered. Paddling with all his strength, the best Sandy could do was to keep us from losing ground. He decided that the only way to make it the rest of the way through the strait was to tow *Piglet*. The job of towing fell to me. I fastened a line to the cleat on the forward deck while Sandy maneuvered close enough for me to jump onto the rocks. He lowered the sails, raised the centerboard and used the boat hook to fend off while I leapt barefoot from rock to rock, pulling the boat forward.

It was difficult and frustrating work, exacerbated by the irregular shoreline, the incoming ocean swells and the jagged granite, covered with barnacles, mussels and seaweed. The bowline was too short for the job, and several times I had to get knee deep in the water to help Sandy get around the larger rocks. It was getting late when we reached the point at Sandy Cove. I got back aboard and we raised the sails. After two more tacks we finally slipped around the point into the cove, our enthusiasm for *Piglet* at an all-time low.

We were further disappointed to see a young couple already attending a campfire on the beach. We had hoped to have the place to ourselves. Sandy said it wouldn't be a good idea to camp on the same beach with the couple, because they would want their privacy. I didn't question his wisdom on this matter. I was only ten. We sailed back out of Sandy Cove and were finally able to make some progress tacking to the south. After several hundred yards we reached Rogue Island, a pile of rock about three hundred feet long. Rogue Island had always held our fascination both for its name, which appealed to us in a particular way, and for its barren exposure to the ocean. It was separated from the shore of Cundys Point by no more than two hundred feet, but from its rugged appearance it could have been ten miles out to sea. The only vegetation consisted of a few straggly conifers, twisted from constant buffeting by the wind, and a thick undergrowth of bay and juniper with a sprinkling of poison ivy.

Sandy and I landed on the north end of the island where we were protected from the wind. The tide was getting high and we were able to unload our supplies and camping gear directly onto the shore without having to struggle over seaweed-covered rocks. Once everything was out of the boat we puzzled over how to secure *Piglet*. We didn't want to leave it on the rocks, but we didn't have an anchor. Sandy solved the problem. We first tied the main sheet (a long line used to secure the mainsail) to the cleat on the bowsprit. I stood on shore and held the end of the line while Sandy paddled backwards to a lobster buoy, which he lifted out of the water and draped over the stern into the cockpit. I then pulled the boat back in, Sandy stepped out and we tied the end of the line around a rock, allowing *Piglet* to drift safely away from shore.

As we set up our campsite we began to realize how ill-prepared we were for overnight camping. We had no dinner, and no pot to cook in, nor anything to drink except the sodas we had bought at Christine's. We didn't have any candles, had neglected to include a flashlight, and didn't even have a spatula for flipping pancakes. Sandy, at least, had thought to bring a book of matches.

Sandy set me to the task of gathering driftwood and building a fire, while he got back into *Piglet* and hauled up the lobster trap that was acting as its seaward anchor. Stealing lobsters is a very serious offense in Maine, and we had never done anything like this before out of respect and consideration for the lobstermen, whose living wrested from the sea was not an easy one. But our situation was difficult at the moment, and the one undersized lobster Sandy found in the trap was not likely to be missed.

I built the fire in a crevice a few feet above high tide. Sandy emptied our coffee into a napkin, filled the can with salt water and balanced it directly on the burning logs to boil. The lobster was unhappy with our efforts to immerse it in the coffee can, and the water that spilled as a result of its struggle nearly put out the fire. But the lobster eventually succumbed, the fire recovered, and within twenty minutes, in the fading light of evening, Sandy and I enjoyed a crude meal of nearly raw lobster and potato chips, followed by roasted marshmallows. When our dinner was over we didn't stay up long. We had no light except from the fire, nothing to read, no games to play—none of the things with which we normally entertained ourselves in the evening back on Sheep Island. So, we made our beds as comfortable as possible on the uneven shore and turned in early.

Neither of us slept well. There was no position on the rocks that was not excruciatingly painful. We had no level ground, no pillows, and no foam mat or air mattress under our sleeping bags to soften the granite pressing into our bones. All night we tossed and turned, and in the damp chill of pre-dawn our sleeping bags were not sufficient to keep us warm. Long before the sun came up we were both huddled in our sleeping bags by the rekindled campfire, crowding so close that we were in danger of catching fire ourselves. But when the sun finally rose it soon coaxed us out of our cocoons and we began preparations for breakfast, the only meal we had properly planned.

The pancakes cooked easily over the open fire, and we took turns flipping them in the pan, inspired by a story our grandfather Blachly had often told of cooking flapjacks for a team of cowhands in western Colorado after his father was killed. One Sunday morning, he told us, he was cooking breakfast when a couple of girls from the neighboring farm came walking down the road on their way to church. In an effort to impress them he flipped a flapjack high in the air and held the pan behind his back to catch it—a maneuver he had practiced many times. But the pancake never came down and he couldn't find it until he went to put his boots on after breakfast. There it was, cooked only on one side.

There is something different about the taste of food cooked outdoors, especially a hot breakfast after a cold and miserable night. Our only regret was that we had no water with which to make the coffee. When we were done with breakfast we tried to douse the fire by peeing on it, but it made such a horrible stink that we finished off the job with a few coffee-cans-full of salt water. We then quickly broke camp. The tide would be high again by mid-morning and the wind had started to come up from the northwest. If we waited too long we would again have to fight both wind and out-going tide on our way back through the Bear Island Strait.

We tacked back to Cundys Harbor but hadn't realized how early it was. Christine's was not yet open. The only activity in the harbor was a lobster boat taking on bait. We continued up river to Sheep Island, moored *Piglet* and made our way up the pier to *Rocky Ledge*. The wind-up alarm clock in the kitchen read 6:55. No one was yet awake, so we wearily climbed the stairs to our bedroom, got into our beds and fell asleep.

The author and his friend, Robby, in 1957 trying to sail the "RP", which they created from the bow of a broken-down rowboat that had washed up on the island. Betsy Boat is visible in the foreground. (Photo courtesy of Rob Miller)

CHAPTER 8:
Betsy Boat

By the time I was ten years old, I could have drawn a fairly accurate chart of most of the islands, coves, inlets, and reefs within a couple of miles of our cottage on Sheep Island. I had spent so much time exploring and playing with my brothers and friends that our knowledge of the area extended to the formations of rocks, the trees, and the ebb and flow of the tides. We knew where to find garnets embedded in boulders on Bushy Island, and where to find bits of mica on the back shores of the Basin. We knew which reefs supported the biggest mussels, and which ones were favored by seals. We knew where veins of white quartz ran through the granite shores. We knew at which tides it was safe to take an outboard skiff at full speed through the back channel to Cundys Harbor, or through the maze of reefs and mud flats at the north end of Sheep Island.

My only independent means of transportation that summer was *Betsy Boat*, an 11' wooden rowboat named after my sister, who had claimed it the day we moved into our cottage three years earlier. *Betsy Boat* was a narrow, flat-bottomed boat with two seats and a classic, sloped-up stern—a design from the turn of the century. It was better suited for the safety of a small pond than the open waters of Casco Bay, but it was easy to row, and though small, was heavy enough to hold its forward momentum between oar strokes. I had learned to row it at age seven, the summer we moved into *Rocky Ledge*.

Betsy Boat had endured a rough and temporary conversion to a sailboat three years earlier at the hands of my older brothers, but the effort had proved unsatisfactory. The improvised keel, an 8' length of 1x12" pine, was ineffective at keeping the boat from sliding sideways in the wind, and the use of an oar in place of a rudder was as frustrating as it was impractical. I was grateful to inherit the aging rowboat as my own after my two oldest siblings, Jim and Betsy, took summer jobs away and no longer spent their vacations on Sheep Island. I enjoyed endless hours on the water, relishing my new independence and mobility.

One Sunday morning I awoke earlier than usual and was struck by an eerie stillness. I propped myself on an elbow and looked out the window. Not one ripple marred the reflection of the pre-dawn sky on the expanse of water before me. There was no wind at all, and no lobstermen yet making their early rounds. Even the seagulls had not begun their daily pilgrimage up the New Meadows from their nesting places on the outer islands of Casco Bay.

I slipped out of bed and dressed in slow motion to avoid waking Sandy and Jon, sleeping in adjacent beds, or my mother in the next room. Our cottage was tiny and built with no sound insulation. The walls and floors were single-thickness wood planking and seemed to amplify every creaking footstep as I made my way, barefoot, downstairs and out the back door. I hoped that whoever heard me would only think I was taking an early trip to the outhouse. But my intentions were much bolder.

I made my way on the pine-needle path around the side of the cottage and down to the pier. The sun had still not risen as I untied *Betsy Boat*, climbed in and shoved off from the dock. Quietly, I mounted the oars in the oarlocks and took my first few strokes, pointing the bow straight across the New Meadows River. Within a few moments I was a hundred yards from shore, watching our cottage, snuggled in a forest of red spruce, growing smaller with every stroke.

The only sounds were the rhythmical shifting of the oars in their oarlocks and the swishing of water dropping from their tips with each backstroke. I was entranced by the reflected image of the island, its perfection marred only by my wake and the swirling

Rocky Ledge in early morning light.

eddies of my oar strokes. When I was halfway across the river the sun rose behind me, turning the trees on Sheep Island a brilliant green. Our cottage shone like a jewel bathed in the morning light. The sun flashed off the backs of my oars and refracted into prisms through the droplets that streamed off their tips. I stopped rowing several times to drink in the scene.

By the time I reached the far shore of the New Meadows I was warm from exertion. I shipped the oars and drifted with the incoming tide into the entrance of the Narrows, a small channel between the south shore of Brightwater and the north shore of Phippsburg. My destination was the Basin, one of the greatest natural harbors on the coast of Maine—surrounded on all sides by land and accessible only through the Narrows. The Basin had served sailing ships for more than three centuries as a safe harbor during storms, and had been a haven for native civilizations for over four thousand years. As the tide rises and falls in the Basin, the current rips through the Narrows with such force that sailing or rowing against it is futile. In the old days the "tall ships" would catch enough wind above the treetops with only their topsails to maintain steerage and maneuver safely past the shoals at the entrance of the Basin. But they had to wait for the tide to make either their entrance or departure through the Narrows.

I coasted along in the shallows of the Brightwater shore, occasionally dipping an oar to keep the bow facing forward. Zephyrs rustled the leaves of the birch trees overhanging the rocky shore. The tide was close to full, and the branches formed a canopy over my head as I drifted beneath them. The cold, clear salt water revealed barnacle-covered rocks and gently waving seaweed below me.

When I entered the Basin I started rowing again, slipping along the far shore, around "Denny Point", and up a tidal inlet that in six more hours would be a mud flat. But at that moment, at the peak of high tide, it was a magical, isolated sanctuary. A great blue heron, surprised by my quiet approach flew squawking from its perch by the water. The whooshing of its huge wings echoed off the shore. A tern darted about, deftly dipping its bill in the surface from time to time to catch its breakfast. Sometimes a vast school of tiny iridescent fish would turn below me in unison, reflecting silvery flashes of sunlight through the water.

For quite a while I drifted in silence, listening and watching dreamily. Eventually, I started feeling hungry, and realized I had lost track of time. The sun was now high in the sky. Everyone back on Sheep Island would be up, and my mother would surely be distressed at my absence. I took up the oars and started for home. As I rounded the point into the main body of the Basin, I found myself rowing against a gusty wind from the south. The Basin was still calm, but I knew that out on the New Meadows things could be different.

My passage through the Narrows on the outgoing tide was fast and easy, but as I came out into the river I was greeted by a stiff breeze from the ocean and a rough, wind-driven sea. *Betsy Boat* pitched diagonally into the waves, and rowing became difficult. As I got further from shore I began to feel unsafe. I did not have a life jacket or even a life cushion. Instead of fighting wind and waves on a direct course home, I decided to take my chances rowing to Dingley Island, about a half mile to the north, reasoning that once in the lee of Sheep Island I would find the wind less severe, and by this triangulated course find my way home. Heading more to the north away from the wind did make rowing a little easier, and I could surf down the face of an occasional wave. It was exhilarating, but tiring, and required great attention to keep the bow from burying itself in the backs of the waves.

After half an hour I reached Dingley Island. But when I turned to the south and felt the power of the wind and the full force of the waves I was alarmed. The wind was so strong that if I failed to feather the oars, turning their blades parallel to the water with each backstroke, they would act as sails and push me backwards. The waves were so large and close together that *Betsy Boat* would lurch over the top of one only to dig her bow into the face of the next. Several times water came in over the bow and before long there was more than an inch of it washing at my feet.

I quickly changed my plans about getting home and determined instead to reach the safety of Howard Goddard's dock on Dingley Island where I could wait for the wind to subside. I glanced over my shoulder to gauge the distance. The dock was not far, but it was fully exposed to the waves, making a parallel landing impossible. A young girl was standing there, holding the railing of the ramp and waving at me dramatically with her free hand, signaling me to come in. I didn't need any encouragement. Within a few minutes I nosed *Betsy Boat*'s heaving bow close to the dock.

The girl knelt quickly, reached for the bow line and managed to get it around a cleat, while I shipped the oars and stowed them under the seat. But *Betsy Boat* now thrashed in the waves like a wild thing at the end of its line, and I had no way to get out except across the bow. I turned to face the dock, hands gripping the gunwales, water washing at my feet in the bilge.

On the next wave I lunged to the bow and struggled to pull myself forward. Just as I grabbed the cleat and rubber bumper on the corner of the dock the boat dove into an on-coming wave. My footing disappeared as water poured in over the bow, and for a moment I was left hanging from the edge of the dock. I scrambled up, no worse for wear except for a soaked pair of pants. *Betsy Boat*, now almost half full of water, wallowed miserably at the end of her line, but there was nothing more to be done until the wind died down. I followed the girl up the ramp to the safety of the granite shore.

Sherry Adams, like me, was ten years old. She was very pretty, with dark blonde hair tied in pigtails. She told me she lived on the far side of Dingley Island next to the causeway that joined Dingley with Great Island. She had been walking by the point when she noticed me fighting my way across the New Meadows, and her

Sherry Adams with Sir Lancelot, 1960. (Photo courtesy of Sheridan Adams)

concern had grown as my boat drew close enough for her to see that I was just a boy. When she went down and stood on the dock and felt the violence of the wind and waves she was convinced that I was in danger. She had been trying to get my attention for some time before I turned and saw her.

We sat down together in a grove of birch and oak trees above the shore. I pointed out Sheep Island and told her of my pre-dawn row to the Basin. She told me about her family and her horse. Our conversation was punctuated by long pauses during which we sat in the warming sun and listened to the wind in the branches above us. Out on the New Meadows the water was green and the tops were blowing off the waves. As we sat there, side by side, looking out to sea, Sherry slipped her hand into mine. For a long time we sat quietly, hand in hand.

Suddenly, Sherry grew nervous, realizing that she had been away from home for quite a while. Worried that her parents would be angry, she let go of my hand and quickly stood up. The wind had died down somewhat, and though the New Meadows was still rough, I assured Sherry that I would be able to get home. We walked back to the grove of trees above the dock and turned to say good-bye. Sherry leaned forward and gave me a quick kiss on the cheek, then turned and ran up the road, disappearing past the corner of an old work shed. I stood there for several minutes with the long grass waving at my knees. Above the sound of the wind in the trees a seagull cried. I turned and walked down to the dock, pulled *Betsy Boat* forward, secured her to the front of the dock and bailed her dry.

Rowing home was difficult, but nothing compared to crossing the New Meadows an hour earlier. The tide had dropped substantially, revealing the many reefs between Dingley Island and the north end of Sheep Island. They acted as a barrier against the wind and sea, and there were only a few places where I had to row in unprotected waters. The last few hundred yards to our dock were the worst, but I hardly noticed. My mind was fully occupied with thoughts of Sherry Adams.

CHAPTER 9:
The Storm

Christine Miller was the first to tell us that some heavy weather was coming our way. As Postmistress of Cundys Harbor and proprietress of Holbrook's General Store she was always a source of information about important happenings around the New Meadows. She had heard a gale warning on the radio that morning and relayed the news when I arrived in my family's skiff to pick up the mail that afternoon. With me was my best friend, Robby Miller, whose family lived in the cottage next to ours on Sheep Island.

The mail run to Cundys Harbor was a kind of social ritual for the six families on our side of the island. Nearly every day someone would go to the harbor for supplies and return with everyone's mail. Distributing the mail was the basis for quite a bit of interaction between adults and children alike, and was one of Robby's and my favorite activities.

Today we had something special to communicate to our neighbors, and we wasted no time getting back from the harbor. As we approached Sheep Island we came on Sandy and Jon sailing in *Piglet* and warned them to get back home right away. It took some doing to convince Sandy that a storm really was coming. The sky was still clear, and in the lack of other evidence it was our earnest excitement that finally convinced him we were telling the truth. When Robby and I reached our dock, *Piglet* was not far behind, sailing "wing and wing" before the wind.

It was not uncommon to have strong winds on the New Meadows. Small craft warnings, with winds up to 30 MPH, were routinely issued by the Coast Guard, even on clear days; but we generally regarded them as invitations to go sailing in *Piglet*. Really strong winds, however, were a different matter. Even a moderate gale with winds up to about 40 MPH could be dangerous, breaking branches and dragging moorings. We were expecting a full gale, with winds that could exceed 60 MPH—enough to uproot trees, tear shingles off roofs, break windows and rip boats away from their moorings. In a full gale, anything not tied or nailed down was likely to be blown away. For the families living on Sheep Island the information that Robby and I were carrying was not to be taken lightly, and we relished the sense of importance it gave us as we ran from house to house, delivering the mail and the news.

By the time Robby and I finished our rounds and got home to our respective cottages, Sandy and Jon had arrived and had already stowed the sails of *Piglet*. My mother heard a confirming report on our battery-powered transistor radio: increasing winds expected from the northwest late in the afternoon, shifting to the northeast and reaching gale strength by evening, accompanied by heavy rain and thunderstorms. Out on the New Meadows the south wind and clear sky still gave no hint of bad weather.

In preparation for the storm there were quite a few things to be done that required everyone's help. My two oldest siblings, Jim and Betsy, had summer jobs away, and my father was still in Washington, DC until the last week of summer. So it fell to my mother, Sandy, Jon and me to make the place ready. Mom quickly made a list of preparations and assigned the various jobs: Sandy and I were to secure *Royal Tern* and get the small boats out of the water while she and Jon brought in extra firewood, got the furniture off the porch and put up the storm shutters, normally used only to close up the cottage for winter.

Sandy and I got some extra line out of the tool shed at the back of the cottage and took the skiff down to the cove where *Royal Tern* was moored about 100 yards south of *Rocky Ledge*. The mooring was anchored by a huge V8 engine block at the end of 30' of heavy chain and had not budged since my father managed to get it into place four years earlier. We thought *Royal Tern* would be safest where she was, but there were a few things that might help her ride out the storm. We tightened the sail-cover on the mainsail, and lashed down the boom, made sure all the sheets and halyards were tightly belayed, and the jib stowed in a sail bag far under the forward deck.

We got out her 20-pound anchor and lengthened its line with the extra rope we had brought with us. After securing the line around the mast and belaying it to the big cleat on the forward deck we took the anchor in the skiff and dropped it about 150' to the northeast, the direction from which we expected the worst wind. We then used the skiff to try dragging *Royal Tern* backwards, both to test the mooring and to get the anchor to "dig in." As a final precaution Sandy checked my knots. All of us were proficient at a variety of marine knots: bowlines, sheep shanks, fishermen's bends, clove hitches, "eye" splices and the like, but Sandy, five years my senior, didn't want to take any chances. Satisfied that we had done all we could, we headed back to *Rocky Ledge*, where Jon was helping Mom get the storm shutters up.

We still had to bring in the small boats, a job made a great deal easier by the high tide. In front of *Rocky Ledge*, at the base of the 10' granite cliff that gave our cottage its name, was a gently sloping stretch of granite that extended from the path by the pier down to the high tide mark. Over this incline Sandy and I brought *Betsy Boat*, then *Piglet* and finally our skiff, lifting and dragging them on wooden rollers. It was strenuous work, but nothing compared to what it would have been at low tide when a great expanse of seaweed-covered rocks dropped twelve feet to the water. Even walking over these rocks was challenging, but dragging the boats up over them would have been really difficult.

We pulled *Betsy Boat* up to the woods next to the house and turned her over. Both *Piglet* and the skiff we left on the path near the pier, about 5 feet above high water, and took the extra precaution of

Storm clouds to the north.

tying them both to a tree. These preparations were very similar to what we would be doing a few weeks later as we closed up camp at the end of the summer. The south wind had died completely in the hour it took us to secure the boats, and there was now an ominous stillness in the air.

When we went down to get the life cushions and other loose items from the dock, dark clouds were starting to move in over Dingley Island to the north. My mother and Jon joined us on the pier to watch the approaching storm. As we stood there looking to the north, gusts of wind started to buffet the water in the distance, kicking it into a patchwork of ripples, and disturbing the glassy reflection of the black clouds above.

Within minutes we felt the first gusts on our faces. The sky overhead turned black and the boats in the cove to our north started swinging at their moorings. The last rays of the setting sun still lit up the shore of Brightwater on the far side of the New Meadows, in stark contrast to the darkness rapidly enveloping us. There was an electric tension in the air, like the day four years earlier when we had capsized in *Royal Tern*. The wind quickly strengthened from the north, bringing with it the first pelting raindrops. We laughed with excitement and raced up the pier to the shelter of our cottage.

As we piled in through the back door, the smell of new rain and wet pine needles accompanied us. We were met by the uneven staccato of raindrops against the wooden walls and the sound of the north wind rattling the shutters. With the shutters on, the cottage was dark and mysterious. It gave me the strange sensation of being an intruder. I went upstairs to get on some warm clothes while my mother lit the lamps in the living room and Sandy built a fire. The rain steadily increased and the wind started to whistle under the eaves.

Alone, upstairs in the dark, with the storm now howling around the eaves, I wished that I had brought a candle with me. I finally found the clothes I wanted, changed, and felt my way back down the stairs. When I opened the door to the kitchen it was like entering a different world. Sandy had lit the Coleman lantern, which generated so much light that it transformed the kitchen into a bright and cheerful place. The smell of sautéing onions and mushrooms greeted me. We were having spaghetti for dinner. My mother asked me to get lettuce and other greens out of the icebox, and I spent the next ten minutes helping her prepare a salad.

As we sat for dinner, the wind howled outside. Conversation was limited to marveling at the power of the storm. After dinner my mother insisted that we all take sponge baths, noting that we smelled of seaweed and mud flats. Although we objected strongly, there was no denying she was right. So, after heating up a pot of water to do the dishes, we heated up a second one with which to bathe.

Our bathing facilities were Spartan. In the washroom there were two antique mirrored dressers, each bearing a large porcelain washbowl and pitcher. Tonight, our bathing was even more perfunctory than usual, for we were distracted by the growing storm. The wind kept increasing, and the rain was coming down so hard that it created a constant din. Water began to seep through the north wall of the cottage, dripping down above the couch. Then, in the distance above the wind and rain, came the sound of thunder.

Flashes of lightning could be seen through the cracks of our shutters. We measured its approach by counting seconds between the flashes and the thunder that followed, allowing 700 feet per second. "That one was a mile away," said Sandy. As the thunderstorm drew closer the tempo of lightning flashes increased and the thunder took on a threatening quality. Soon it was right on top of us.

The lightning crackled everywhere, accompanied by deafening peals of thunder that rattled our little cottage. We sat by the front windows, peering through the cracks in the shutters to see what might be revealed by the brilliant flashes. But rain was coming down so hard we could see nothing past the posts and railings of the screened porch.

Gradually, the thunderstorm blew past us. By the time we went to bed the sound of the thunder was fading into the distance. For some time after my brothers and I blew out our lamp my mother sat in bed reading by candlelight in the next room, the light reflecting dimly off the wooden ceiling as we drifted off to sleep.

I was awake again at the first light of dawn. The house was silent. There was no sound of rain on the roof, no howling wind. A few rays of sunlight found their way through cracks in the shutters, lighting up dust particles that drifted slowly above me. I slipped out of bed and crept silently down the stairs and out the back door. The ground was soaking wet, and the pine needles stuck to my bare feet. Mist was rising in places from the forest floor.

Our boats were unharmed, though they were more than half full of rainwater. I went down and checked the dock, which was littered with seaweed. but I could find no damage. *Royal Tern* was riding low in the water, but her mooring had held. Unfortunately, the extra anchor line had twisted around the mooring line and it took some time to untangle it. The only indication of the storm's ferocity was that much of the seaweed had been torn from the rocks in front of *Rocky Ledge*, and some of it had washed onto *Royal Tern*'s foredeck.

Later that morning, after removing the shutters and taking advantage of the high tide to get our boats back in the water, I ran over to Robby's house where I helped move some porch furniture back outside. After helping bail out his skiff and getting it into the water, the two of us went exploring, looking for evidence of storm damage around the island.

The family at the north end of the island had lost one of their skiffs. Its broken bow line was still dangling from their dock, securely fastened to the cleat, but there was no sign of the boat. We found it a few hours later, beached on the Cundys Harbor shore. The Sargent's cottage had lost a few roof shingles but the rest of the homes on Sheep Island were fine. Across the river on Brightwater, we heard later, a huge white pine had fallen on a log cabin, doing considerable damage.

Most of the storm damage on Sheep Island was limited to fallen trees, especially on the thickly forested south end of the island. Robby and I found one tree between our two cottages that had been split by lightning. The top part of it was suspended at a sharp angle high overhead, precariously held in place by the branches of adjoining trees. Robby and I had been hoping for something much more dramatic: a pier blown away, a boat staved in, or a house struck by lightning would have suited our adolescent lust for excitement. As it was, the storm's legacy was little more than several days' worth of work clearing fallen trees and cutting them into firewood. Sandy summed it up for us. "*Piglet* weather," he joked, lamenting that the storm had not taken place during the day so we could go for an exciting sail.

The author with Sherry Adams and Sir Lancelot, 1960.
(Photo courtesy of Sheridan Adams)

CHAPTER 10:
Sherry Adams

"What have you been *doing*?" my mother asked in an accusing tone. She could see that I was trying to hide something. She was good at that, although she often overstepped her intuition, presuming I had done things I hadn't. This time, however, there was no escape. She had seen me emerging from the bayberry bushes by the pond on Dingley Island just as she drove up on her return from Brunswick. Worse, I was followed by my friends Sherry Adams, Donna and Charlene Blackwell, Maggie Duffy, and Rob Miller, all looking sheepish and evasive. I was too innocent to attempt a brazen lie, but managed to play for time. "Nothing," I said, hurriedly grabbing a bag of groceries and starting toward the shore. I knew it was futile to avoid the truth, but I only wanted to be spared the embarrassment of confessing in front of my friends.

My mother was "old school", born in 1911 and raised in a prosperous section of Montclair, New Jersey, as the eldest of seven children in a home steeped in both classical culture and rigid Presbyterian doctrine. She was a talented pianist, an avid reader of English literature, was deeply religious, and had been teaching school in Florida in 1940 when she met my father, seven years her junior. Married later in life than most of her siblings, she didn't have her first child until she was 30. When I was born she was 38, significantly older than the mothers of most the other children with whom I grew up. And she, much more than my father, was the authoritarian parent who provided most of the discipline for her children.

"*Peter*," she continued as she followed me down the ramp to the dock, "I know you were up to something."

"Oh Mom," I answered, "It was nothing." My voice had a complaining edge to it that said by its tone that I was too old and independent to be badgered and embarrassed by my mother. But she was not to be deterred. I was only eleven and still very much under her watchful eye—or so she thought.

"You all looked guilty—what were you doing in those bushes." I could see that her imagination was conjuring up extreme images, and that the truth might be a relief.

"We were just playing 'Spin the Bottle.' Didn't you ever do that?" I demanded, mimicking ever so slightly the accusing tone she had used on me.

"I don't like…" she began, but stopped herself. I had won, but it was an uncomfortable victory. I helped her get the groceries into the skiff, then untied the bow line and held the boat for her while she stepped in. "I want you home by five o'clock," she said. "We need some firewood cut and brought inside."

"OK, mom," I answered obediently. "Thank you," I added as she started the motor and powered away from the dock. That was lucky, I thought, for she could have made me come home right away. As it was, I still had several hours to spend with my friends.

Our game of Spin the Bottle had served its purpose: we six boys and girls had broken down the self-conscious barriers of adolescence and had exchanged kisses—partners randomly selected by the impartial dictates of an old soda bottle. But some of the spins had been calculated. Both Sherry and I had managed to manipulate the bottle so that most of the time it would point to each other. Thus, we had found a way to accomplish in a ritualized manner what we both wanted but were too shy to do on our own. They were awkward kisses. The first time I leaned across the circle at the bottle's command we were both smiling nervously, and instead of contacting Sherry's lips I found myself kissing her front teeth. But the ice was broken, and despite the teasing laughter around us, the glances we exchanged confirmed what we both knew: Sherry and I had crushes on each other.

I hurried back up to the shore and found Sherry waiting for me. The rest of our friends had continued up the dirt road towards Maggie's house, so we were alone. "Is everything OK with your mother?" she asked. She was clearly upset at having been discovered, and was only slightly reassured when I told her how I handled the situation. "I hope she doesn't tell my parents." The thought worried her, and she dwelled on it in silence for a moment before brightening up with a suggestion that we go for a row in *Betsy Boat*.

It was a perfect idea. This way we could be alone. *Betsy Boat* was ideally suited for two ten-year-olds. We slid easily through the water as I rowed around the south point of Dingley Island. The tide was high and had transformed the narrow mud flats on the back side of Dingley Island into a serene and expansive inlet. The surface was unmarred by even a ripple once we rounded the point into the protected waters. "I know a really neat place we can go," said Sherry. "It's kind of a garden." We rowed and drifted along the shore until she pointed out a break in the rocks. I nosed *Betsy Boat* in, shipped the oars and pulled us the rest of the way under an overhanging bough. We found ourselves in a hidden grotto.

"This is the first time I've come here in a boat," said Sherry in hushed tones. "It's real hard to get here through the woods." We were not more than 200 yards from Sherry's house, but the woods along this shore were thick with undergrowth. I held the boat while Sherry stepped out, then followed her onto the uneven rocks. I tied the bow line to a tree root and noted that we might have less than an hour before the out-going tide would strand our boat on the rocks. I followed Sherry, scrambling up to the forest floor over a steep embankment of soft black earth. When I reached the top she was already seated, facing me with her back against a giant spruce.

"What do you think?" she whispered. I was impressed. The place she had led me to was like a secret bower. It was a small clearing—not more than 15 feet across, ringed by ancient red spruce that towered sixty to eighty feet above us. Here the forest floor was carpeted with thick green moss that shimmered wherever the sunlight reached it. Pale green patches of "British Soldier" lichens with tiny spots of ruby red accented this vast living carpet, interrupted only by a large, irregularly shaped boulder in the center of the clearing. "I like it," I whispered.

Sherry and I talked and played together innocently. We made up stories that seemed to fit with our magical surroundings, about elves, and unicorns, and dragons. We examined the different shades of mosses and lichens, the texture of the bark on the trees, and watched the resolute efforts of an ant carrying a leaf. We talked a little about our families and compared the routines of our daily lives during the school year. I envied her for living in Maine year-round, for having her own horse, for having a father with a sports car and speedboat, for being the oldest of her siblings.

I thought Sherry's life must be heaven compared to mine. I was the youngest of five, had to be at school by 8:00AM each morning, had daily choir rehearsals and services to sing at the Washington National Cathedral, including two on Sundays. I had two hours of mandatory sports every day, an hour of piano or classical guitar practice, and up to three hours of homework every night. Further, most of my toys and clothes were hand-me-downs from my three older brothers, while Sherry, being the oldest, got the first and best of everything. "But you have your own boat," she countered, "And you can go anywhere you want."

We had been so absorbed in talk and play that we didn't notice the change in the air until Sherry noted that it was getting chilly. The sun had grown dim behind a thin veil of clouds. I looked up and saw misty tendrils wrapping themselves around the trees. "Fog!" I stammered, slightly alarmed. Then I remembered the boat. We had completely lost track of time. The tide must have gone out a long way by now. I bounded to the top edge of the embankment. *Betsy Boat* was below me with her bow pitched wildly into the air, her bow line stretched tight and her stern resting in mud. She was firmly aground.

"You're going to have to help me," I said. I didn't even know how we were going to get the bow line untied, it was under so much tension. Sherry and I climbed down the embankment to examine the predicament more closely. *Betsy Boat* was only eleven feet long, but the front five feet of her was suspended in the air. I asked Sherry to stand on the other side of the boat, and together we tried to move it forward to take the tension off the bow line. But at this angle the wooden rowboat was too heavy for us. I suggested that we both get inside and jump up and down in the bow, hoping that the extra weight would force it down, thereby pulling the boat forward just a little. This strategy worked. I untied the line, and working together we were able to get the boat back into the water. But the fog had come in so thickly that I couldn't see the opposite shore, less than 50 yards away.

When we were finally seated and I had the oars out, Sherry worried about the fog. "It won't be any problem getting around to Goddard's dock," I reassured her, "because we can stay close to shore." But I didn't know how I was going to get back to Sheep Island. Further, I had the uncomfortable feeling that it was already past five o'clock, the time I was supposed to be home. I began rowing hard. Sherry sat quietly, huddled against the damp. Within ten minutes we had rounded the south point of Dingley Island, and soon pulled up to the dock.

I insisted on walking Sherry home, even though she encouraged me to get back to Sheep Island. "I can't row in this fog, anyway," I said. "When the tide goes out a little further I can follow the reefs, but right now I'd probably get lost and drift out to sea." She accepted my reasoning, but seemed unduly nervous. "I'm afraid my parents are going to be upset with me," she confessed as we started walking.

"Not with me there," I suggested, feeling confident that her parents would afford me a modicum of social amenities as a guest, and that Sherry, at least temporarily, would be protected from any serious trouble. I had often used this tactic with my own mother, knowing that she was always cheerful and friendly around strangers and guests. Early on I had observed that she would switch her mood instantaneously to present her most pleasant side to anyone outside our family. The ring of the telephone or doorbell had rescued me from so many scoldings that "saved by the bell" had a special meaning for me. In my naiveté I assumed that all adults were the same.

But I didn't know Sherry's parents. I had seen her father only once, zooming by in a beautiful speedboat with a brand new 35hp Evinrude, the most powerful outboard motor available at the time. He and his wife were younger than my parents. They looked youthful to me, so I assumed that they were "cool."

As we drew close to her house, Sherry pulled on my hand, urging me to stop for a minute. We were on the back of a slight rise in the road, and when we sat down all but the roof of her house was hidden from view. This would be our last moment alone, I realized. Sitting side by side on the edge of the dirt road we hugged each other awkwardly. The warmth of her body next to me was strange and wonderful. Then we kissed, and everything seemed to dissolve into a tingling happiness. I had never felt like this. I wanted it to last forever.

"Come on," Sherry urged, pulling away, "I'm going to be in a lot of trouble." I stood up and took her hand. I wanted to tell her how I felt, but the words didn't come and I said nothing. As we walked in silence the last 100 yards to her front door I felt an inexplicable heaviness descend on us. I was sure that Sherry had felt the same elation that I did. But her mood had changed, had darkened like the deepening gloom around us.

Suddenly the front door flew open. A glare of light from inside stabbed towards us in the mist, and Sherry's father hovered in the doorway. He was glaring at us, but for half a moment said nothing. There was something very peculiar about his hesitation. I stepped forward and tried to introduce myself. "Hello, Mr. Adams. I'm..." But he ignored me.

"Where the hell have you been?" he demanded of Sherry. There was something wrong with his voice. "You get your ass in here right now," he bellowed. I was too shocked to be afraid, but I could see Sherry was terrified. She didn't answer, only stepped forward cautiously and tried to sidle past him in the doorway. He gave her a rude shove on the back of the head and she tumbled out of sight. Then, without once looking at me, he turned and slammed the door.

For a few moments I stood there in the dark and the swirling mist. I could hear violent, muffled voices from inside, then pounding footsteps. Sherry had been sent to her room. I turned and walked a few yards, then stopped and looked back, hoping to see a light go on in her upstairs room. But I didn't know which window was hers, and no light went on. For several minutes I stood there, caught by longing and confusion. Finally, full of misgivings, I waved good-bye to the upstairs windows of the angry house and walked away into the gloom. It was getting quite dark before I got home that evening, but I blamed my tardiness on the fog. Although she was upset and worried, my mother didn't dispute the explanation that I had to wait for low tide so that I could follow the reefs back to Sheep Island.

It was a week before I saw Sherry again, and it came about in a strange way. My mother, returning from town one day told me that she had run into Sherry's mother, and that I had been invited to come over for a visit. I had an uneasy feeling that our parents were setting up an "appropriate" social context for Sherry's and my friendship, but I didn't mind. I was just glad for the chance to see her again. Since the incident with her father I had been afraid to even try. I was sure that her parents were as angry with me as they had been with her. I didn't conceive until much later that Sherry's father might have felt remorse for his behavior, or might not even remember it. However, I was pleased to suddenly find myself the object of many friendly overtures from both her parents.

Over the next several weeks Sherry and I spent a great deal of time together, often in the context of some family activity. Jim, her father, took us water-skiing several times, took us for rides in his Porsche roadster, and generally acted like a benevolent uncle to me. Sherry's mother was gracious and friendly. I joined the family for picnics and afternoon swims and was even invited one night to sleep over.

But there were inexplicable rifts in the fabric of this seemingly happy family life. Sometimes when I came to visit, Sherry's mother would barely greet me, or ignore me entirely. There were days when she stayed in her bedroom with the shades pulled and didn't even come downstairs. From time to time I would overhear heated words coming from inside the house, or see Jim angrily spinning the wheels of his Porsche, kicking up gravel and dirt as he sped out of the driveway.

Gradually, Jim seemed to start favoring me over his own children. When we were out in his boat he would sometimes let me steer, a privilege I accepted, arrogantly assuming it was just because I was the only boy in a sea of girls. One day as I arrived at the house he came out and diverted me from even saying hello to Sherry by showing me something fascinating about his car. But the worst was the day Sherry and I were planning to go on our own picnic, when Jim intervened and invited me, and me alone, to go fishing with him. It was an offer I did not want to accept, but felt I could not refuse. I suggested that Sherry should come with us, but he replied that this trip was only for the men. Sherry followed us to the dock, and I could see the look of envy and betrayal on her face as we pulled away. I felt helpless and miserable.

A week later came the event that troubled me the most. I had joined Sherry's family for a boat ride and picnic out to Rogue Island. The day started well enough. The weather was perfect. Everyone seemed happy, and we all helped with the picnic lunch and loading of the boat. But shortly after leaving the dock Jim's mood grew dark. Everyone else was talking and laughing, but he was silent. I didn't notice until we were almost to Rogue Island, when he started giving orders for our landing. There was a harsh tone in his voice, and every word sounded like a scolding. As we were unloading our supplies on the shore, he exploded at Sherry for setting the radio down on the sand. "Goddammit," he bellowed, "Where were you when God passed out the brains? Don't you know sand will ruin the transistors?"

There was a stunned silence. Sherry looked like she had been slapped across the face. Her mother, trying to act like nothing had happened, started giving unnecessary instructions to Sherry's younger sisters. Jim went back to get something from the boat, and Sherry walked numbly in the opposite direction until she rounded the point and was hidden by the brush. I followed and found her sitting forlornly, looking down at a puddle in the rock. Tears were rolling down her cheeks, and she didn't look up when I sat down beside her. We sat there silently for a long time. I put my arm around her shoulder but said nothing.

Eventually, Sherry's mother came around the point. "Here's some hamburgers, children," she said as if it was any other happy day. I took both hamburgers and thanked her. She glanced nervously at Sherry, who still hadn't looked up, then turned and walked away. I finally ventured to speak. "It's not your fault," I said. "I didn't know sand would ruin a radio, either." Sherry turned only slightly and rested her left hand on my knee.

"What's wrong with him?" she asked through her tears, not expecting an answer. "I don't know," I ventured, "He's angry about something." She shook her head.

"It's the beer," she said conclusively, as if she had heard it said before. She had certainly seen it too many times, I realized.

I had seen adults at cocktail parties get happy and talkative, but had never witnessed the power of alcohol to transform someone into an indulgence of anger and coarseness. I was too innocent to understand the full gravity of the situation, and was reluctant to admit that an adult could have a *problem*, especially someone who had been as kind and generous to me as Jim. But the evidence was compelling, and Sherry's tears made it very real for me. "It'll be OK," I tried to comfort her, but my voice betrayed my lack of confidence.

The rest of the family had all gone swimming. We could hear them laughing and playing in the water. After a long time, Jim appeared from around the bushes. "Come on over here, Snipe," he called out softly, using Sherry's nickname. His voice had lost its hard edge and Sherry responded. She stood and walked over to him. Jim put his arm around her gently and said, "Let's go home."

Sherry and I continued to see each other for several summers, but after Rogue Island we tried to avoid doing anything with her parents, and we never talked about it again.

CHAPTER 11:
Fire on Ragged Island

The summer of 1961, when Ragged Island burned, I had a classmate from Washington, DC visiting me in Maine for a couple of weeks. Don lived only a few blocks from me in Chevy Chase, Maryland, just outside the District line, and we usually took the same bus home from school. Like me, he was a boy soprano in the National Cathedral Choir. His father also sang in the men's section as a bass. I often rode home with them after late-night Friday rehearsals and Sunday afternoon services, so Don and I spent a lot of time together. Don's father usually smelled of alcohol, but seemed nice enough.

Don was not prepared for the kind of life we led on Sheep Island. He had grown up in the DC suburbs and had never even been camping. His idea of excitement was a trip to the movie theater or amusement park, or watching a re-run of *The Thing* on late night TV. He didn't enjoy the absence of electricity, telephones, and hot and cold running water, and it was quite evident that he found our simple lifestyle primitive, boring, and stupid.

I had some difficulty adjusting to the pressures his attitude put on our friendship. Even in play he was cynical about the things I found engaging. He had no interest in rowing and he didn't have the patience to appreciate the finer points of *Betsy Boat* or the antics of fiddler crabs in their borrowed periwinkle shells. He thought *Piglet* was ridiculous, was obviously uncomfortable at having to sit close together in the cockpit, and didn't like sailing anyway. The suggestion to go exploring in the woods of the uninhabited south

The author (on right) with Don McCandless, his classmate and fellow choirboy from the Washington National Cathedral, 1961.

end of Sheep Island was brushed off as childish until I told him with enthusiasm that I had once heard a moose in the woods.

The first thing Don did seem to enjoy was running the outboard motor. I taught him the simple controls of the 3-horsepower Evinrude in about 30 seconds: the choke, the sliding throttle lever, the steering handle and the starter cord. It was similar enough to his family's lawnmower, with which he was intimately familiar, that he mastered the mechanical aspects with ease. The problem of landing at a dock took a little longer for him to overcome, but not much damage could be done with only a 3hp motor, and I was relieved to have found something that Don seemed to like about being in Maine.

Unfortunately, his enjoyment of the outboard was short-lived. The satisfaction he at first derived from the sense of domination over Nature was quickly replaced by his scorn at the pathetic speed of our skiff. We were putt-putting along at full throttle when Sandy

Sargent zoomed by in his speedboat at more than 25mph. Don's face lit up as he witnessed the potential for speed and power illustrated by Sandy's boat, but his expression changed when it occurred to him that our under-powered skiff would never deliver that kind of excitement.

After Don had been with me for a few days our friendship was strained almost to the breaking point. I kept hoping to find something that he would enjoy. I tried "borrowing" my parent's car and driving it around the dirt road on Dingley Island. That got his attention, stealing cars being an activity that seemed to appeal to him, but it was a risky endeavor. I could barely reach the pedals of the big '56 Chevy wagon, and though I was fortunate enough not to have an accident, I received a such a scalding look from Mrs. Blackwell as we drove past Howard Goddard's house that I was intimidated into giving up the idea. We parked the car and decided to take the skiff up to Cundys Harbor.

The Harbor had slightly more appeal to Don than Sheep Island, due to the availability of candy and cigarettes. He was too young to get away with buying cigarettes over the counter, but when we got into the boat after leaving Sid Watson's store he revealed an entire carton of Larks that he had managed to steal while I paid for the gas and oil. I had mixed feelings about this turn of events. Like most of my schoolmates I had not been above stealing an occasional candy bar at the local drug store back home in Washington, but stealing a whole carton of cigarettes from Sid didn't go over well with me. However, I held my tongue in deference to our fragile friendship.

We then proceeded up to Christine's to collect the mail for Sheep Island. That year Christine had opened up a snack shop on Holbrook's Pier. The menu consisted of typical coastal snack bar foods like cheeseburgers, French fries and soft drinks, as well as local specialties: deep-fried clams, crab cakes, and lobster rolls. The food was a welcome alternative to the wholesome meals provided at home. But more important to my circle of friends was the function the snack bar served as a social center. Christine employed

Watson's General Store

young people to run the place, and my best friend Rob Miller and I often found ourselves the beneficiaries of favoritism displayed by her mostly teenage, female staff. When money was short, which was most of the time, we could sometimes procure, for no more than the asking, a hamburger bun with all the fixings except the hamburger—a handout rationalized by the fact that such an item was not on the menu and didn't fit the definition of a real hamburger.

But Don didn't fit in with this crowd, and for the two weeks that he was with me I had little contact with my other friends, and I didn't presume to take undue advantage of my special status with them. Before going up for the mail, therefore, we bought, and actually paid for—with spending money Don had brought with him—two cheeseburgers, an order of fries and two cokes, which we wolfed down in complete silence. Finally, we walked up for the mail.

Christine greeted us in her usual amiable way, seeming to accept Don as if he were a part of my family. Since we had just arrived by boat, she asked us if we knew about the fire on Ragged

Island. We hadn't heard anything about it, and asked her tell us what was happening. Starved as we were for excitement, we received the information with great enthusiasm. Then, with impulsiveness and spontaneity natural to our youth, we thanked Christine and raced back to the boat, anxious to get out to "Raggedy" before all the action was over.

It took us nearly two hours to go the five miles from Cundys Harbor to Ragged Island. Don's enthusiasm for the venture started to fade as soon as we got into the open water past Rogue Island when I was able to point out Ragged Island on the horizon, still four miles away. He did perk up a little at the sight of black smoke rising from the heavily forested island, but his attitude continued to sour in direct proportion to the size of the swells we met as we passed between Flag Island and Long Ledge. By the time we got to the south side of Ragged Island Don was feeling seasick and angry.

The main part of the fire had already been extinguished when we arrived to join the firefighting—a good thing, considering that we were hopelessly ill-prepared for taking part in any such effort. We were barefoot and in short pants and t-shirts. We had no gloves, no eye-protection, and not even any sunscreen. On top of that, we were only eleven years old. Nonetheless, we found somebody who seemed to know what was going on and volunteered our help. Incredibly, he gave us each an "Indian tank," which we strapped onto our backs. He then sent us up the charred hillside towards the woods to put out "hot spots."

From what we could learn, the fire had started next to the house near the water's edge and had burned rapidly up the vast grassy field that dominates the southern face of the island. It had then jumped the stone walls that crisscross the field and had gotten into the trees, though it didn't appear to us that very much damage had been done to the forest.

The soil on Ragged, as with most islands in Maine, was a loamy peat of decomposing spruce needles. In places it was smoldering several inches deep. Don and I picked our way along, watching for telltale signs of smoke or glowing embers in the ground. Being barefoot we were probably the best hot spot detectors among the thirty or forty volunteers on the island. We spent the entire afternoon scouring the upper fields and neutralizing hundreds of glowing embers with streams of water from our Indian Tanks.

Don was a small boy, several inches shorter than me, but extremely muscular. Even at eleven he had well defined biceps and had amazed the entire school that year by doing over fifty chin-ups in the Presidential physical fitness tests. He worked tirelessly, refilling his tank 15 times or more during the course of the afternoon. Those tanks were heavy, weighing about 40 pounds when full, and I was impressed with his unflagging commitment to the job for which we had volunteered.

Occasionally he would take a cigarette break, which I thought was pretty ironic considering what we were doing there. For some reason he had brought the entire carton of cigarettes onto the island. After a few minutes of struggling with the Indian Tank he opted to leave the carton on a stone wall while keeping one pack with him. A few hours later, as we were getting ready to call it a day he went looking for his carton of Larks and couldn't find it anywhere.

After asking around we finally found someone who knew about the missing cigarettes. It was local boy in his late teens. He said that all the fellas thought the cigarettes had been left there for the volunteer firefighters by the people who owned the island. He said that everyone had enjoyed those cigarettes all afternoon and were feeling mighty grateful to the person who left them on the wall. Don wasn't very happy with this report, but I was secretly satisfied, feeling that there was a certain divine justice at work in this turn of events.

It was quite late in the afternoon when we finally put down our Indian Tanks. We were exhausted, dirty, and famished, having eaten nothing since leaving Christine's. Down at the landing there was an amazing jumble of boats, but the thing that immediately caught my eye was the unmistakable shape of a Coast Guard utility boat. These fast, all metal boats were reminiscent of the old PT boats from World War II. They had a dynamic deck line that started low at the stern and leveled off towards the bow. There was something distinctly military in their appearance. We didn't often see them on the New Meadows, and they generally elicited from us about the same response one would have at the approach of a state trooper with flashing lights.

As Don and I stumbled down to the shore to find our skiff a Coast Guard sailor approached and asked if one of us was named Peter. I froze. No matter what circumstances had led to this question, I figured it wasn't good. I swallowed hard and answered yes. "You boys better come with me," he said. Don and I were both ready to die. Were we being busted for the cigarettes? Had we forgotten our life cushions? We followed the sailor to his boat. He instructed us to come on board and had us sit on the rear deck to wait for a senior officer. I asked him what was going on.

"Your mother has been calling us for the past several hours, and we just want to get word back to her that you're OK." said the sailor. Don and I relaxed considerably. There were no phones on Sheep Island, so Mom must have gotten a neighbor to take her up to Cundys Harbor and called from Christine's after finding out from her where we had headed in the skiff. The senior officer approached, saying he had just left a message for my mother at Holbrooks Store that we had been found at Ragged Island and that we were all right. He asked me if our skiff was OK. I told him it was fine. He asked where it was and I pointed it out, nestled between a 32' lobster boat and a big Westpointer. In this company the skiff looked especially small and unseaworthy. The 3hp outboard motor on the stern looked like a shrunken head. I felt ashamed for it. The officer considered the boat for a moment, looked us over and said, "How would you boys like a tow home?"

As soon as we accepted the offer the crew began preparations for our departure. At that point it dawned on me that their appearance on Ragged Island had nothing to do with the fire. The Coast Guard was there for the sole purpose of finding me and Don and getting us safely home. I speculated that our lives were going to be in more danger back on Sheep Island than they had been all afternoon, but I let the thought pass. Don and I got the skiff and brought it around so that it could be tied to the stern of the boat, and within a couple of minutes we got under way. We felt a thrill of excitement as the engines roared to life. The whole hull vibrated with the sound and we felt infused with the engines' massive power. When the captain put it into gear the big boat leapt forward. The bow line of our skiff snapped taut behind us, shaking off drops of salt water that sparkled in the late afternoon sun.

When we got away from shore a few hundred yards the captain increased our speed. I kept my eye on our skiff and watched apprehensively as it surfed down the face of our huge wake and almost swamped as the bow dug into the water. The captain had been watching for this too, and immediately slowed down so that one of the sailors could tie on a longer line. When we got under way again our skiff was trailing thirty feet back and was able to ride in the center of our wake with its bow high above the water. Much to our delight the captain poured on the power to get us home before dark, and for some time Don and I stood at the stern marveling at the size of the wake behind us.

About half way to Cundys Harbor one of the sailors offered us a sandwich. As we devoured it he asked us questions about the fire and about our trip out to Ragged Island. We had to shout to make ourselves heard above the roar of the engines. During the afternoon the swells had grown considerably and until we got to Bear Island we had to steady ourselves by keeping a hand on the boat. I was glad we didn't have to spend another two hours bringing the skiff back home through these waves. It would have taken us well past dark. I was also grateful for the sandwich and the friendly demeanor of the Coast Guard crew. But mostly I was happy to have done something with Don that I knew he would remember enthusiastically for years to come.

CHAPTER 12:
The Mystery of the Islands

Malaga Island lies darkly to the east of Bear Island, only a mile from *Rocky Ledge*. It has been uninhabited for more than a century, and is completely overgrown with thorny brush, juniper and poison ivy beneath a thick canopy of red spruce. No one lives there, and though it is separated from the shore of Sebasco by only a few hundred feet, few people ever visited. One overcast day Don and I went there to explore. I had sailed and rowed past it many times, and had always been taken by its foreboding presence. Today, with a chilly northeasterly wind blowing offshore across the Sebasco channel, the impression of mystery was enhanced, and we felt a rush of excitement and fear as we stepped into the forest at the water's edge.

Within a few feet the trees closed in around us, and we found ourselves struggling to make progress through heavy underbrush. The rustling branches and snapping twigs under our feet sounded unusually loud—so loud that we stopped every step or two to make sure that ours were the only footsteps in the forest. But we could hear nothing except the wind whistling strangely in the treetops. It sounded different than the wind on Sheep Island, like a low moaning from a forgotten time. We said nothing, but exchanged glances, daring each other to proceed.

After a few more steps we came upon an ancient shack buried in the trees. The doorway was partially blocked by a young spruce, and the door hung wildly, held only by its bottom hinge. There was a single window with most of the panes broken. The unpainted wooden walls were weathered black and severely rotted, with moss and lichen reaching up from the ground. "Let's check it out," whispered Don. He stepped forward, pushing past the branches blocking the door, and disappeared inside. I followed into the gloom and was greeted by the pungent smell of decay.

There may have been a wooden floor here once. Now there was nothing but rot and humid black soil. I expected to see some sign of earlier habitation, like an old calendar hanging on the wall, or a broken chair discarded in a corner, but there was nothing in this ruin to hint of its former inhabitants. Don picked up a small rock and threw it at the only remaining pane of glass in the window. The sound of shattering glass fell strangely on our ears, followed by an even stranger silence. I looked at Don and signaled with a nod towards the door that we should leave. He nodded in agreement, like me unwilling or unable to speak out loud or even whisper in the oppressive confines of this decaying place.

We pushed our way out the door and struggled though the brush for several yards until the shack disappeared behind us. "That was scary as hell," I said out loud, trying to prove to the spirits of this place that I would not be intimidated. "Damn right," answered Don, his voice sounding as hollow and scared as I knew mine had. The wind still moaned overhead, and the forest around us appeared more impassable with every step, like a seamless wall of green. "Let's get out of here," I said, reduced again to a whisper. Don nodded, and we started pushing our way towards the shore, making sure that we gave the shack a wide margin. I thought that we had gone a long way into the forest, but it must have been only a few yards, for in just moments we burst out of the woods onto the shore. There we were stopped in our tracks by a loud and authoritarian voice, "Hey! You boys!"

Ten yards to our right a lobsterman was working on a pile of traps. He glared at us menacingly. We looked at him in dumb anticipation. "You're not allowed to play around here," he continued. "Don't you know this place is haunted? Now get on out of here."

Without another word he turned and went back to his work. Don and I looked at each other and shrugged, then climbed down to our boat and headed home. We didn't go back to Malaga after that, and it wasn't until many years later that I started learning about the mysteries of the place.

More than a century ago Malaga Island was home to a community of about ten families, comprising some forty adults and children. Their houses were ramshackle affairs, and though some of the residents tried to tend small gardens in the acidic soil, the people of Malaga depended for food almost entirely on what they could catch in the surrounding waters of Casco Bay. By the turn of the century there were no trees left on the island, for they had all been cut down and burned for firewood. Some of the islanders appealed to the town of Phippsburg for help, and records show that the town fathers did at first offer a pittance. But the help was grudgingly given, for the people of Malaga Island were not only poor, they were also mixed race, descended from Benjamin Darling, Sr., a formerly enslaved person.

By the early 20th century the white townspeople of Phippsburg considered Malaga Island a disgrace to their community and a detriment to the growing summer tourist trade. Further, they did not want the financial responsibility of providing welfare for its residents. At one point they tried to disown the impoverished community by claiming the island belonged to the town of Harpswell on the other side of the New Meadows River. When that tactic failed they appealed to the governor and began a campaign of public pressure through the local press.

Reporters from Bath visited the island several times during the first ten years of the 20th century and reported that its inhabitants lived under the most horrendous conditions. One reporter claimed that everyone on Malaga was so filthy and unkempt that he "doubted any of them had ever seen a bar of soap." But the most damaging rumor propagated by the press was that the residents of Malaga were mentally retarded. In New England during the developing industrial age of the late 1800's, poverty and "feeble-mindedness" were often equated in the eyes of the puritanical middle class.

Another reporter claimed that the island community was organized as a monarchy. This fallacy was based on a misunderstanding of an old local custom. It was common along the Maine coast in those days for the best fisherman in a community to be called "King" in recognition of his accomplishments. The public, however, seemed eager to believe any outlandish report about the islanders who had turned Malaga into a local eyesore. Finally, in 1912 the governor, under pressure from the local townspeople, took possession of the island, cleared off the residents and leveled or burned the houses.

In the years that followed, local imaginations ran wild, and the history of Malaga Island was quickly shrouded in myth. When my father was a boy in the early 1930's he had heard that the US Navy removed the islanders during World War I out of concern that they would offer assistance to German submarines. Even in the early 21st century many local people held the belief that the residents of Malaga were descended from the black concubines of sea captains returning from Africa. Others still said the islanders had a King. And it remained a common belief that the community was in-bred and the people "feebleminded", as they called it in those days. But these stories appear to have been manufactured to cover the town's shame and guilt at the abysmal treatment afforded the Malaga Islanders.

In the mid 1800's Benjamin Darling, Sr. apparently bought Malaga Island and lived there with his family. Over the years his children intermarried with white families in Sebasco and Harpswell. Many of them built homes and lived on Malaga. The community was constantly in flux, with families and individuals moving on and off the island every year. Darling's son, Benjamin Jr. married a white woman from Cundys Harbor and lived on Sheep Island in the late 19th century. They had seven children. It is hard to imagine what their life on the island must have been like through the harsh winter months. "Summer people" purchased Sheep Island in 1907, and most of the cottages, including *Rocky Ledge*, were built within the next four years. The Darlings were gone and forgotten, leaving behind only the mysterious ruins of their house, the foundations of which my brothers and I discovered in an overgrown clearing at the south end of the island in 1957. None of us knew at the time that Sheep Island and Malaga Island shared this common heritage. But we sensed something odd, almost supernatural, about both places, and it wasn't just the scary feeling of the woods.

Something strange had also happened at *Rocky Ledge* many years before we got there. Perhaps someone had died, or some tragic family argument had occurred, but in the middle of the summer of 1935 the cottage had suddenly been deserted. It was not an organized departure. The cottage had not been closed up, and nothing was cleaned or put away. The closets and bedrooms were left full of clothes. The beds were unmade. The kitchen was left with food on the stove, the dishes unwashed. Even toothbrushes and other toiletries had been left behind. The cottage stood this way for more than twenty years until my parents discovered it. Unable to locate the owners, they eventually paid the back taxes and moved in.

When we first arrived on Sheep Island in the summer of 1957, the house was like an archeological find, with an otherworldly feel to it. Aside from their personal belongings, the only trace of the former inhabitants was a list of names and dates recorded in fading pencil on the north wall of the living room. Two names in particular stood out: Eleanor C. Low and Bobby Hoagland. Eleanor's name appears several times with consecutive dates as far back as 1922. Bobby's name starts appearing in 1927. By 1932 their names appear together as Robert and Eleanor Hoagland. The last entry was in 1934. Nobody on the island seemed to know much about the former inhabitants of *Rocky Ledge*. Fran Sargent, who had been on the island at the time, told me before she died at the age of 103 that she only remembered the family had two daughters, but the reason for their sudden departure was a mystery to her, too.

As long as I could remember I had felt uneasy when alone at

The outhouse at Rocky Ledge in 1987. The author and his brother, Alex, celebrate having successfully moved the old outhouse a few yards to a new location.

Rocky Ledge—even in daylight. And at night, especially in the dark of the woods behind the house, I was always gripped with fear. After dark I seldom went more than halfway up to the outhouse, and I would usually sprint back to the house in terror, feeling safe only when the kitchen door had slammed shut behind me.

Chapter 12: The Mystery of the Islands

On our first day at *Rocky Ledge* in 1957, Jon and I went exploring with our new friend and next-door neighbor, Robby Miller. Robby and I were seven. Jon was ten. We started out together, but near the middle of the island decided to split up, agreeing that we would get back together later and share our adventures. Robby and I went off together across the island while Jon headed toward the south end. As soon as we had separated Robby and I started feeling uneasy. We kept hearing strange sounds in the woods, and within minutes we were lost. We spoke only in whispers and tried to tiptoe silently. But a sudden noise—we thought it was the bellowing of a moose—terrified us into a run.

We ran wildly, crashing through the underbrush, until the woods opened up on the rocky shore at the west side of the island. Once in the open we felt safer, and decided we would get back home by going around the island on the rocks instead of through the woods. It took us a long time. In places the rocks were too steep to be passable and we had to make detours into the woods to get around. Every time we entered the forest we were filled with the same inexplicable dread.

Jon was having a similar experience, only worse, since he was alone. He still had not gotten back home when Robby and I finally reached *Rocky Ledge*, and a half hour later my father and two oldest brothers went out searching for him. They found him an hour later, sitting on the rocks at the southern-most tip of the island, staring out to sea. When my father asked him why he was sitting there, Jon said that that he had been so scared of the woods that he wasn't going anywhere unless someone came to find him, and that if no one showed up he would wait for high tide and drift out to sea and drown.

Later that summer Sandy and I found what looked like the foundation of an old house and a well in a clearing just past the cove where we moored *Royal Tern*. There was nothing left of the house; just a rectangular rise on the forest floor, covered with moss. The well was only about three feet deep, but some of the stonework was still intact. There was a second foundation in the fern patch behind *Rocky Ledge*, but no one on the island knew what house had stood there, or who had lived in it. Of all the places on the island, these two were the scariest, even during the day, and we avoided them unless there were two or more of us together. In the dark the entire island felt so scary that not once during our childhoods did any of us venture to camp outside overnight.

In 1971 I went to Sheep Island for a week in May to rebuild our pier, which had been carried away by a winter storm. I had gotten married the previous summer to a young yoga student at the behest of my yoga teacher, an Indian Yogi whom I regarded at the time as a "spiritual master" or Guru. My new wife and I were only 18 and 20 at the time, idealistic, impressionable, and more enamored of our Guru than of each other. After a rocky year of marriage we were now alone on the island, but it was no honeymoon. We both felt the same sensations I had experienced as a child: that there was some kind of presence there. On the first day I cut down several trees with which to build the crib for the new pier. That evening as dark descended on the island, I was gripped with a great uneasiness, which rapidly grew to a state of terror. The air felt thick and there was no place, even inside the house, where either of us felt safe.

I built a fire in the Franklin stove and we huddled around it, too terrified even to go into the kitchen to make dinner. The energy grew even more intense. I felt ashamed to be so afraid, but could not shake the feeling of utter dread. It was so bad that I even tried praying. We both did. We sang chants we had learned in yoga class. I tried speaking out loud to the "spirits of the forest," asking forgiveness for cutting down the trees. We prayed to the ghosts of *Rocky Ledge*, telling them we meant no harm. But the terror persisted, and neither of us could move from our place by the fire. Finally, close to midnight just as we were running out of firewood, the feeling shifted. It was so sudden that my wife and I looked at each other in surprise. Then we laughed with relief. There was no explaining these feelings, but we had no doubt they were real, and for the rest of our stay we were left in peace.

But on dark nights I sometimes still feel the presence of something at *Rocky Ledge*, and wonder if it is the ghost of one of the Hoaglands, or perhaps the spirit of Benjamin Darling, Jr., looking after his lost home on Sheep Island.

Note: Malaga Island is now owned and maintained as a historical site by Maine Coast Heritage Trust.

In the summer of 1959 Zack Longley and "Sandy" prepare for another day of waterskiing, this time having remembered their bathing suits.

CHAPTER 13:
Waterskiing in the Basin and Other Pranks

Across the river to the east of Sheep Island lies the shore of Phippsburg, a long peninsula stretching twelve miles from Bath out to sea to its southernmost termination at Small Point and Popham Beach. Along its jagged western shoreline are numerous coves, islands, and inlets that provide harbors for fishermen and shelter for mariners, as well as potential for exploration and adventure for bold, curious, and stouthearted youth. All the boys of Sheep Island fit this description. But in addition to such nominal virtues, other more questionable qualities were manifest in the characters of my brother Sandy and his friend Zack Longley. They were devilishly mischievous and prone to undertake impulsive and outrageous escapades—especially when in each other's company, which was a lot of the time. As the tag-along little brother, I was often witness to their pranks, sometimes a participant, and just as often a victim of them.

A couple of incidents during the summer of 1959 stand out in my memory. The first may seem small in retelling, but it was so archetypically representative of Zack's behavior and has been retold with gleeful delight so many times over the years that it has become part of the island's mythology. There are no roads or sidewalks on Sheep Island, despite a 1908 survey that showed pretentiously named boulevards and streets encircling and crisscrossing the island's 10 acres. Instead, there was a well-worn footpath linking the cottages on the east side of the island, and a single, overgrown path between our cottage, *Rocky Ledge*, on the east, and the Longley's camp on the west.

One sunny day Zack and Sandy were crossing the island on their way to some adventure, with me in tow. Midway across, out of sight of the cottages, both "big" boys (they were 14) stopped to relieve themselves into the bushes. I followed suit, but took a little longer, and was still in the middle of the operation when Zack and Sandy had already re-zipped their pants, impatient to be on their way. "Wait for me," I pleaded as they crossed behind me. At that very moment the little devil that has always lived on Zack's left shoulder must have whispered something in his ear, for he was overtaken by an impulse to give me a sudden shove on the back, landing me face down in the wet bushes. Zack and Sandy laughed gleefully at this mischief, even as they helped me back to my feet. "I'm sorry," said Zack through his guffaws. "I just couldn't help myself!" Zack was never mean-spirited. He was a friendly and equal opportunity prankster whose mischievous laughter was inclusive and understood by his victims as his unique way of expressing friendship. In other words, he could get away with behavior that in anyone else would be considered bullying. Apparently, I was a pretty good sport about it, too, which explains in part why he and Sandy allowed me to accompany them for other delinquent activities.

The Basin is a fantastic saltwater "lake" directly across the river from Sheep Island. It is, of all the features of the Phippsburg shoreline, the most inviting and interesting. At high tide its deep coves and inlets, which are mudflats when the tide is out, become perfect places for swimming, rowing, fishing and—if you are a 14-year-old boy in possession of a skiff with a 16-horsepower Firestone outboard—water skiing! Zack was just such a 14-year-old. One day at high tide Sandy and I piled into Zack's skiff and headed across to the Basin with a pair of water skis and a length of rope for a towline. We navigated through a fleet of expensive pleasure craft anchored in the middle of the Basin, past Basin Island (where eagles now nest each year), up a long inlet and past an outcropping of rocks that

Chapter 13: Waterskiing in the Basin and Other Pranks

100 years earlier had been the site of a tidal saw mill. There, in the furthest reaches of the cove, we landed at a rocky point to make our preparations. It was only then that Sandy revealed he had forgotten to bring a bathing suit.

Zack and Sandy joked for a moment about the possibility of skiing naked, but opted instead for a more modest approach. Sandy quickly fashioned a short skirt of seaweed, held in place by a piece of twine around his waist. Thus attired, he elicited a solemn promise from Zack, who would be driving the skiff, that he would not venture past Basin Island into the area where the fleet was anchored. Zack dutifully agreed. I was left sitting on the shore, because, with only 16 horsepower, any extra weight would compromise the boat's ability to pull a skier.

There are a couple of different ways to get up on water skis. The driest way, once you know how to do it, is to start by standing or sitting on a dock and jumping forward onto the water just as the boat is gaining speed and the ski line is going taut. The other way is for the skier to float in the water with ski tips up, the towline between them. When the line goes taut the driver guns the engine and, with luck and some skill, the skier gets pulled up and out of the water. We were well practiced in both methods, but in the absence of a dock at the far recesses of the Basin, Sandy had to do a water start. What he had not counted on was the effect that being pulled through the water at high speed would have on his skimpy attire. By the time he was up on the skis, most of the seaweed had been dragged off the twine and Sandy was almost completely naked.

Sandy gestured wildly for Zack to turn back, but it was too late. With uncommon glee, Zack steered the skiff straight out past Basin Island and dragged my hapless brother right through the center of the anchored fleet. Sandy, unwilling to let go of the towline, made the best of it as pieces of seaweed continued to fall off his waist. As I sat waiting for them to return, an elderly woman meandered down the path behind me with her granddaughter, a small girl about my age. Not noticing me, they sat on a bench by the water's edge about 20 feet away. Within a moment or two I heard the whine of Zack's outboard and looked up to see the boat rapidly approaching, with Sandy 60 feet behind, still up on skis and now with only one strand of seaweed left, and that one not very advantageously placed.

As they drew near it was plain to see that Zack was quite pleased with himself, especially when he noticed the elderly matron and her ward seated on a bench just a few yards behind me. To make matters worse, Sandy, not knowing what was ahead, dropped the towline and skimmed to a stop right in front of them, his naked body fully exposed as he sank into the water. The old lady was livid. As Zack circled back and Sandy pulled himself over the gunwale butt-naked into the skiff, she hid her young charge behind her skirts and let out a most un-lady-like stream of four-letter words in a thick down-east drawl, ending with a threatening "We've got some boys in Sebasco who know how to take care of the likes of you!" before storming away, dragging her curious granddaughter by the arm.

A couple of years later Zack and Sandy and the other older kids on the island went off for summer jobs, then college and careers. For years after that I rarely saw Zack, but I am happy to say that he has not changed. Even though, as adults, we find ourselves on opposite ends of the political spectrum, we share a mutual fondness, addressing our political differences with the kind of mock abuse that only good friends can get away with. During the Presidential campaign of 2008, for example, I planted an Obama campaign sign on his front lawn and sent him a photograph of it, eliciting a very satisfying stream of invective.

Zack never did follow through with the threat with which he tormented me for years: that he was going to take a can of paint and change the name on my mother's sailboat, replacing the "n" in *Royal Tern* with a "d." One of these days, however, if he's not careful around me, he might find himself face down in some wet bushes.

CHAPTER 14:
Uncle Clarence's Poetry and Other Summer Reading

On long summer evenings there was not much to do on Sheep Island. With no television or radio, and long before the ubiquity of cell phones and other addictive devices, our options were to play cards or board games, do some knitting (my mother taught all her children to knit), or read a book. *Rocky Ledge* came stocked with a small collection of aging hardcover volumes, most of them from the late 1800s and early 1900s. Among this collection we found a treasure of delights in a book of humor titled "My Demon Motorboat" by George Fitch. It was published in 1912 in the early days of motorboating and tracks the misadventures of two midwestern landlubbers, lifelong best friends who try to outbluff each other as experienced boatmen when they are, in fact, totally ignorant of all things nautical.

Written in a style reminiscent of Mark Twain, the two friends mercilessly taunt and berate each other with sarcasm while bumbling through a learning process that includes just about every idiotic mistake it is possible to make on a motorboat. After purchasing a boat together, then delaying for weeks while pouring untold amounts of money into repairs, the two set out on their first adventure, which included such missteps as tossing the crank overboard, casting off from the dock before starting the engine, and—after drifting a mile or two down the Ohio River—finally getting the one-lung engine started backwards by spitting in the carburetor and wrapping the battery in a life jacket. Their return to the dock, running up river in reverse, cemented their reputation among the local boating crowd, with the dock attendant declaring in frustration that they should retain the services of a nurse.

Sandy would read these passages aloud, sending us into fits of laughter that left our bellies hurting. And it went on for years. Every summer we would re-read the book from cover to cover, sharing it with any guests and friends who came to visit. My brother was so taken with it that years later he often spoke about it with his students at the University of Notre Dame, where he was a professor in the Music Department. Several years back, one of his students found a copy on line and presented it to him for Christmas. I then found a couple of others, and we now own several copies, distributed among family members throughout the country, with one copy each at *Rocky Ledge* and the *Field Cabin* for the entertainment of future generations. But there were other sources of literary amusement for our summer evenings, as well.

One of my grandfather's seven brothers was an elegant looking gentleman named Clarence Dan Blachly. We called him Uncle Clarence. He was tall, strikingly handsome, and extremely intelligent. He spent most of his career in the US Department of Commerce, and had authored several scholarly works, including a definitive treatise on U.S. tariffs, and a 1920 tome bearing the cumbersome title "The Treatment of the Problem of Capital and Labor in Social-Study Courses in the Churches". But after his wife, Margaret, died in 1954 at the age of 72, Clarence seemed forever lost in a torment of unrequited love, though his longing for love and affection may have started much earlier. He and Margaret never had children—the family joke was that they didn't know how—so Clarence was left alone in the world after her death. To woo the opposite sex, or perhaps to give vent to his considerable frustration, he focused on his lifelong avocation of writing poetry. Lots of it.

Uncle Clarence was wedded to the artform and considered himself to be one of the brighter stars in the firmament of renowned poets, on a par perhaps with Wordsworth, or Dickenson. Ezra Pound might have been a more appropriate point of comparison, for much of Clarence's output was little better than doggerel. His high sense of self-esteem as a poet, therefore, was mostly unwarranted, and left him vulnerable on many fronts. His primary downfall was his ardent belief that he was blessed with his own personal muse, and that any words his muse might choose to speak through his pen must remain inviolate and be left exactly as they first came out. He therefore refused to edit a single line or stanza, and would take no advice from anyone regarding the quality of his considerable poetic output. Some of his earlier works are actually quite good, and my father often said that if Uncle Clarence had only trusted an editor to toss out ninety-five percent of what he wrote, he might have been considered a respectable minor poet. But Clarence couldn't refrain from publishing even the most trivial bits of verse, such as this deep-thinking observation:

Clarence Dan Blachly, the author's great uncle, about 1925

"The Greatest Poets"

The greatest poets here below
Tell you what you already know.
(From *Word Pictures of the West, Vol. VIII*)

Unwilling to consider editorial advice, and unable to find a commercial publisher who felt as highly about his poetry as he did, Uncle Clarence used a portion of his government salary to self-publish volume after volume of the stuff. There are nine separate volumes of *"Seasons and Days"* published between 1949 and 1959, and several of *"Word Pictures of the West"* published in 1960 and 1961. He would print 1,000 hardback copies of each volume and send them, unsolicited, to community and university libraries around the country, or give them away as birthday and Christmas presents. A few years ago, while sorting through my father's effects, I found a large manila envelope labeled in Clarence's hand *"Unsolicited Praise for Seasons and Days"*. The contents were mostly polite, hand written letters of thanks from librarians in small midwestern towns I had never heard of.

Most of Uncle Clarence's earlier volumes are dedicated to his wife, but later works bear dedications to various other women, including Princess Margaret on the occasion of her 1958 visit to Canada. But the dedication that stands out from the rest is to a woman named Ilse, in Volume II of *"Word Pictures of the West"*. So taken was he with Ilse that he also wrote and published another paperback booklet of love poems entitled *"Poems to Ilse"*. This little volume with a light blue cover provided untold hours of entertainment for my siblings and me during long rainy evenings on Sheep Island. We would open the booklet—or any of Clarence's many volumes—at random and read aloud to each other, breaking into hysterics at the convoluted sentence structures, forced rhymes, arcane turns of phrase, and maudlin sentiments. Sometimes they had surprising and disturbing endings:

> **"To Margaret"**
>
> The changing colors of the skies
> Are your eyes;
> The wild rose by the creek
> Is your cheek;
> The ocean waves that curl and flair
> Are your hair;
> The coo of doves above the rafter
> Is in your laughter;
> The mariposa lily of the West
> Is your breast;
> But the snows where the rimrocks start
> Is your heart.
>
> (from *Word Pictures of the West, Vol. IX*)

Chapter 14: Uncle Clarence's Poetry and Other Summer Reading

In the summer of 1962, my mother hired a couple of carpenters from Cundys Harbor to rebuild and expand the front porch of *Rocky Ledge*. My next-older brother, Jon, and I were the only children left at home that summer, for Alex (formerly Sandy), Brett (formerly Betsy), and Jim (ages 16, 18 & 19 respectively) had summer jobs away. Each weekday morning, we would await the arrival of our carpenters by boat, and while they enjoyed a cup of coffee before starting the day's work, Jon and I would entertain them by reading aloud selections of Uncle Clarence's poems. We had several volumes of it on our cottage bookshelf, so we had no difficulty finding the most insipid poems and reading them with great emphasis on the forced rhymes and meter. My mother expressed her frustration that the carpenters were thus delayed in getting started on their work each morning, but Jon and I were greatly amused by it. However, we weren't prepared for the fact that the carpenters were innocent of our sarcasm and actually liked the poetry. They were delighted by the simple sentiments. We responded by giving them several volumes of *Seasons and Days*, which they gratefully accepted, saying they would add them to the collection of hymnals and Bibles at the Cundys Harbor Nazarene Community Church, where they were parishioners. I think this was one of the poems that our carpenters liked the best.

"I Knew A Chap"

I knew a chap who always spoke
Like life was nothing but a joke,
Whatever happened or befell,
He had a funny tale to tell.
No matter what the frown or gaff,
He always met it with a laugh.
What was my sorrow, when one day,
I read that he had passed away,
And now a resident of hell's
I wonder at the tales he tells
About the people of the earth,
The subjects of immortal truth.

(From *Word Pictures of the West*, Vol. VIII)

Uncle Clarence's hoped-for affair with Ilse did not have a happy ending. She was substantially younger than he, and, according to my father, was attracted more to his money than to the man himself. After a long courtship, Ilse finally agreed to take a road trip with Clarence to Florida. In preparation for what he thought would be a permanent move and a life-long relationship with his beloved lady friend, Clarence sold his house in Takoma Park, Maryland, and disposed of all but the most necessary of his worldly possessions. Although his beautiful 1950 Packard Deluxe Super Eight was still a very respectable vehicle, he sold it and bought for the trip a brand-new, metallic-blue 1959 Pontiac Bonneville coupe. With Ilse in the passenger seat and their suitcases in the trunk, the happy couple left DC going west on Route 66. But within a few miles, Clarence's erratic driving so unnerved Ilse that she angrily demanded he pull over at a gas station, where she got out of the car, retrieved her suitcases from the trunk, and sent him on his way alone.

With no purpose left in driving to Florida, no possessions, and no home, Clarence eventually showed up at the front door of our house in Chevy Chase, heartbroken and dejected, asking my mother if he could stay with us for a while until he sorted out his life. Thus, Uncle Clarence became an intimate part of my family, and lived for about a year in the bedroom vacated by my oldest brother, Jim, who was away at college. Clarence was a very kind and gentle man, but quite depressed. He would not joke, rarely smiled, and spent most of his days wrapped in a plaid wool blanket, sitting in front of an electric heater at the end of our dining room table. For my tenth birthday he gave me a copy of *Word Pictures of the West - Volume II*, with a dedication scrawled in a wobbly hand. This little volume contains one of my favorite and most-often read of Clarence's poems:

> **"White and Blue"**
> White and blue.
> That is the mountains and that is you.
> White are the snow-drifted summits

Chapter 14: Uncle Clarence's Poetry and Other Summer Reading

And blue are the distant hills
And the sky that spills
Its azure over the forests of spruce,
And blue are your eyes, Ilse, and your loose
Blouse shows your throat and shoulders white
But your bosom is too fair for sight.
White and blue and fresh and cool
Are the mountains like an Alpine pool,
And I always remember the white and blue
Mountains, Ilse, when I think of you.

While he was with us, Uncle Clarence joined us for meals and was always effusive in his praise for my mother's cooking, which was, in fact, quite excellent. Almost every dinner ended with him complimenting my mother on the quality of the meal, as well on her amazing ability to cook "just exactly the right amount" of food. Although it was true that not a scrap of anything was ever left, with the exception of the time she tried to serve us cow's tongue, all of us kids didn't think it was even close to the right amount. We were perpetually hungry and could easily have eaten twice what she prepared. Performing our assigned after-dinner chores, clearing the table, scraping, washing, drying, and putting away the dishes, we would often raid the breadbox, trying to sate our prodigious appetites with odd combinations, like a slice of bread with ketchup. We didn't realize that Uncle Clarence had a different view of hunger.

"When With Hunger"

When with hunger you are tried
And eat, then you are satisfied,
But oh, my Dear, when I adore
Your beauty then I love you more.
I thought that after I had spent
The days with you and as time went
The beauty of your lovely eyes,
The witchery of your thighs,
Would wear away and I would grow

Accustomed to your sculptured brow
And to your little hands that tied
A knot to keep me by your side.
But as the days and hours flew
I became more in love with you,
So much more tender than at first
I fear my heart will burst.

(from *Word Pictures of the West, Vol. VI*)

Clarence had spent his youth in abject poverty and once chided me gently for putting too much butter on my toast. "We didn't have butter when I was growing up," he told me. But he didn't explain why. Perhaps those early memories were too painful. He was only eleven when his father was shot and killed by bank robbers. For the next decade the family faced epic challenges that were especially hard on Clarence's artistic temperament. According to his next older brother, my grandfather, Clarence was never one for physical work. My grandfather was barely 13 when his father's murder left him in charge of supporting his mother and seven brothers. He wielded his authority with such zeal, pushing the boys to work as hard as he did at the physically demanding tasks of survival in the untamed mountains of western Colorado, that his siblings dubbed him the "Slavedriver."

All the hard work did pay off, however, and eventually all eight of the Blachly boys managed to attend college, and several of them, including Clarence, went on to get PhDs in various subjects. But with the poverty and delayed educations, none of the boys married young. Clarence was 35 when he married Margaret Bacon. His mother, "Dellie", about whom much has been written, effused that Margaret was "the perfect wife for Clarence". But what we know of their lives together provides a few hints that

Frederick Frank Blachly, the author's grandfather, about 1950.

the relationship may not have been a very warm one.

Margaret was a strong-willed, proud, and professional woman, a librarian at the Library of Congress, and she had some peculiar ideas about health and lifestyle that she rigidly enforced. For example, she would not allow Clarence to drink coffee or tea. Instead, she would serve him a cup of warm water each morning. He would drive them both to work, and after dropping Margaret off at the Library of Congress, would head to the nearest coffee shop for some caffeine and a blueberry muffin before continuing on to the Department of Commerce. With no children and only a modest house in Takoma Park, they lived frugally, putting away every penny. The result was that Clarence was a millionaire by the time of his death, though his Protestant religious upbringing would never allow him to trumpet the fact. However, neither his wealth nor his outpouring of poetry brought him happiness, for he was an exceedingly lonely man, occasionally prone to morbid introspection:

> **"Self"**
>
> I put my troubles on the shelf
> But could not get away from self.
> I wandered over land and sea
> But could not get away from me.
> You can divorce a wife
> But with yourself for life
> You have to live. Oh wretched luck
> With such a fellow to be stuck!
> (from *Word Pictures of the West, Vol. IX*)

One cold day in December, as I was walking home from school, my attention was caught by the flashing lights of an ambulance, two blocks ahead of me in front of our house. I picked up my pace, but the ambulance pulled away before I could reach it. My mother was reluctant to tell me what had happened, but finally explained that Uncle Clarence had "accidently" swallowed a whole bottle of Aspirin. At the time I didn't fully understand what that meant. The next day Clarence was back home, more depressed than ever, and life went on as before.

Having Uncle Clarence live with us must have been hard on my mother, but she was always kind to him. In gratitude, when he eventually moved to Silver City, New Mexico, to live with one of his younger brothers, he left us his Pontiac Bonneville and promised my mother that she would be the sole heir of his considerable estate. He lived another decade, and in the intervening years was contacted by a development officer from Grinnell College in Iowa, which he had attended from 1899 - 1903. Promised an entire shelf in the college library dedicated to his many volumes of poetry, Uncle Clarence succumbed to the flattery, forgot about his earlier promise to my mother and, in a tribute to his vanity, turned his entire fortune and all his papers over to his alma mater.

My mother was deeply hurt by this, not so much because she needed the money, but because she considered his broken promise quite a slight after the care and kindness she had shown him in his time of need. When I contacted Grinnell a few years ago, seeking more information about Uncle Clarence, there was no shelf in the library dedicated to his poetry. In fact, they could not find a single one of his books, and no more than a few scraps of his papers, which an embarrassed librarian photocopied and sent to me. So much for Uncle Clarence's legacy at Grinnell! Yet his poetry lives on, and his books can sometimes be found for sale on the internet. A couple of his better poems were even turned into songs and recorded by Aaron Nathans and Michael Rondstat, Linda Rondstat's nephew. But the bulk of his creative output still provides endless fodder for family entertainment on rainy evenings in Maine.

CHAPTER 15:
The Hydroplane

By age twelve I was dreaming of speed. Our family skiff in 1962 was powered by a 5-1/2 horsepower outboard, a big improvement over the 3 horsepower Evinrude we had lived with for five years. But it was still pathetically slow compared to the powerboats owned by most of our neighbors. Sandy Sargent had a succession of speedboats, each one faster than the next. The Showells at the north end of the island had a brand-new "MFG" runabout with a 35-horsepower outboard. The Longleys, on the back side of the island, had a ski boat with a 30 horsepower Mercury, and a 16 hp Firestone outboard on their skiff. Each year boats on the New Meadows got faster as the outboard motor manufacturers increased the power of their new models. I was tired of having one of the slowest boats on the river.

One rainy day in April, while waiting with my mother at a Chevrolet dealership in suburban Maryland, I found an advertisement in *Popular Mechanics* hawking plans for an 8' hydroplane. I instantly fell in love with the little boat in the accompanying photograph and thrilled to read that even with a 3hp engine it could skim the water at more than 10 MPH. I could almost feel the boat beneath me as I dreamed of flying up the river with our 5-1/2 on the back. My mother tried to discourage me, but I sent away for the plans, and from the moment they arrived in May I was fixated on the idea of building the boat. All I needed was about $40 for lumber, fittings, and paint.

I immediately began saving my allowance, and by the time we got to Maine that June I already had $18. Robby Miller and I found work with Dotty Showell, each earning $1.00 per hour clearing dead trees and brush from her property at the north end of the island. Within a couple of weeks I had the money I needed.

The author in his hydroplane, 1962

Again, my mother objected, saying the hydroplane didn't look safe. But after taking good measure of my industry and determination she finally relented. The next day I accompanied her to Brunswick, a trip I usually avoided at all costs, and bought two 4'x8' sheets of 1/4" exterior plywood, two 10' planks of 1"x8" pine, a bottle of waterproof glue, an assortment of screws and fasteners and one can each of white and red marine paint. The big sheets of plywood were tied to the luggage rack on top of our station wagon, and my mother had to drive home slowly to keep them from ripping loose.

As soon as we got back to Sheep Island I went to work. I laid out the plywood and scribed a semicircle with a 2' radius at one end, then cut along the curved line with a hand saw. I cut a notch as directed, then bent and fastened the two edges together so that the circular end bent up about three inches, creating the bow. I then cut the braces, sides, and transom from the pine 1x8's. Slathering glue all over everything, I fastened the pieces together with brass screws. Since we had no electricity or power tools, everything had to be done by hand. Drilling holes and putting in the screws by hand took forever, even with Robby and my brother Jon helping, so I didn't get the hull completed until the following day. But by the next afternoon I had the boat finished and painted, sitting on a couple of rollers to dry.

Even my mother had to agree that the little hydroplane looked pretty sharp. It was all white except for the triangular side panels, which were painted fire engine red. Robby, Jon, and I spent the entire afternoon and evening admiring it from every possible angle, speculating on how fast it would go, and trying to think of an appropriate name for it. We could hardly wait for the paint to dry.

The next morning at high tide we carried the hydroplane over the rocks and set it in the water. The paint still hadn't completely dried and the white came off on our hands, but we could wait no longer. The hydroplane sat like a pancake in the water, its bow barely an inch above the surface. My mother looked on with growing apprehension. We then took the outboard off the skiff and mounted it on the transom. This was an awkward job because the 8 inches of freeboard at the stern of the hydroplane was not enough to hold both the motor and the two boys needed to get it in place. The first time we tried, water came in over the stern and almost swamped the tiny cockpit. My mother, witnessing this little incident, nearly cancelled the whole operation, but we solved the problem by having one of us sit on the bow while the other two got the motor in place.

After the motor was secured and the safety chain snapped in place in case the motor worked its way loose from the transom, I started it up. But when I put the motor in reverse to back up, water washed in over the stern. This was going to be trickier than I had imagined. I bailed out the cockpit, put the motor in forward, maneuvered away from the dock, and opened up the throttle. The bow rose up in the air as if it was going to take off, but nothing much happened. Even with the engine opened up full I was barely moving. For a moment I thought there must be something wrong with the motor. Then I tried leaning forward to bring the bow down. Suddenly the little boat jumped up and leveled off into a plane.

I had never imagined the 5-1/2 could whine like that. It sounded like a jet engine as I skimmed along at over 20 miles per hour with the nose of the hydroplane barely three inches above the water. The excitement was unbelievable. I raced around for a few minutes, experimenting with turns and straight-aways, then brought the boat back to the dock so that Jon and Robby could have a try. We spent all morning and half the afternoon doing test runs, running through several gallons of gas, until my mother made us put the motor back on the skiff so that she could go up to Cundys Harbor. I offered to take her in the hydroplane, but she wisely refused. The only way the little boat could carry more than one person was for the passenger to sit on the foredeck. It was not a very secure arrangement, even when standing still.

Over the next few days I found myself negotiating constantly for the use of the motor. Every time I took the hydroplane out it meant that my mother would be stranded on the island. If she was going to town, which she did every second or third day, she would take the skiff, which left me without a motor. On those days I was relegated to *Betsy Boat*, or *Piglet*, both of which were now much less attractive alternatives. This struggle went on for about three weeks until Jon got the idea of buying another motor for the skiff. We pooled our resources: a total of $165.00 (mostly Jon's), and bought a 1955 15 horsepower Evinrude.

My mother was aghast. The ragged old motor was so big she could barely start it, and it was too heavy for her to tilt. When it *was* tilted it would leak gas all over the boat unless she remembered to relieve the pressure in the gas tank, which she rarely did. But the motor was wonderfully powerful and fast. It pushed our flat-bottomed skiff along even faster than my hydroplane, and was so much fun to drive that Jon volunteered to be Mom's chauffeur whenever she needed to go anywhere.

This arrangement worked out especially well for me, for I no longer had to remove the 5-1/2 from the hydroplane every time I was finished zooming around. Unshackled as I was from the demands of my mother's schedule I started using the hydroplane as a utility boat, taking it on longer and longer forays: Cundys Harbor, the Basin, Sandy Cove, and even the Sebasco Resort, where Robby and I had discovered that there were many girls our age on vacation with their families. The next few weeks were idyllic. I could get to any of my usual haunts in no more than eight minutes. This meant that I could have more time with my friends, which at twelve was for me a fact of inestimable importance. Robby and I started spending more and more time visiting the girls at Sebasco. We were pleased to find that in their company we could also take advantage of the facilities at the famous seaside resort. We swam in the private pool, played golf—or at least hacked away at golf balls—hung around the snack shop, and generally made ourselves at home.

One day I went to Sebasco alone in the hydroplane and spent most of the afternoon there. During the day the wind came up strong, and by the time I was ready to leave at around 4:00 PM there were whitecaps visible in the harbor. Even at the back of the dock where I had tied up, the water was rough. When I came down I found waves washing over the bow of my hydroplane and the cockpit full of water. Fortunately, the boat had been designed with three watertight compartments to keep it from sinking. Bailing out the cockpit, however, was complicated by the waves that kept trying to wash in. A number of adults, including the harbormaster, looked on while I struggled to get the water out. I could see they were incredulous. One old woman whispered hoarsely to a friend, "I'd never let *my* grandson take a boat like that out in this weather." Her comment only filled me with bravado, and I made a conscious attempt to appear casual, as if I was used to going out in hurricanes.

Once the cockpit was bailed dry I buzzed away from the dock at full speed, the little hull slapping at the waves and throwing spray to all sides. I continued along the inside of Harbor Island and Malaga Island with the throttle wide open, and finally past Bear Island at the west end of Sebasco. But when I got into the open waters of the New Meadows River, the waves from the south were huge. I had never had the hydroplane out in this kind of weather before. I pulled back on the throttle and tried to ride the waves. I did pretty well until I got near the Sheep Island Ledge in the middle of the river. There a particularly large wave picked me up and sent me surfing out of control down its face. I saw what was coming, but too late I backed down on the throttle.

The nose of the Hydroplane caught the back of the next wave, dug in and buried me. I almost tumbled over the bow as the little boat came to a sudden stop, but was thrown back as water washed completely over the boat. The hydroplane was at a standstill, wallowing with the cockpit full of water, and I was really scared. Then another wave washed over me and threatened to capsize the boat. Incredibly, the engine was still running. I gave it a burst of power, backing off a little to keep the water in the cockpit from washing completely over the engine casing. As it was, the rear deck and most of the motor was under water. But at least I was moving forward, and within a few seconds much of the water had drained out over the transom. The three watertight compartments had kept me afloat.

The wind was whistling past me, and spray from the white caps kept getting in my eyes. I sat low in the cockpit and gave the engine just enough power to ride the back of a wave, keeping the bow high in the air. The boat was still half full of water, but by holding this position I was able to make forward progress and keep from swamping. When I finally got back to Sheep Island I couldn't even land at our dock, for it was too exposed to the waves rolling in from the ocean. Instead, I went around to Robby's dock in the cove, tied up and bailed the boat dry. Then I ran home and changed my clothes before my mother got back from Brunswick so she wouldn't know what danger I had been in.

Near the end of the summer, Jon started taking more of an interest in the hydroplane. He had gotten tired of being at my mother's beck and call, even though he still got a thrill from driving the 15. One day while I was out sailing in *Piglet* with Sherry Adams, he did something I hadn't even dared think about: he mounted the big Evinrude 15 on the back of the hydroplane. The motor was so

Chapter 15: The Hydroplane

Menagerie of Blachly boats at Sheep Island, 1962. From left to right: the author's hydroplane, Betsy Boat, the family's flat-bottomed skiff, and Piglet

heavy that unless Jon sat far forward in the cockpit water would come in over the transom. I am not quite sure how he managed it, or how he was able to avoid my mother's watchful eye. But as Sherry and I came about on the far side of the river we saw a line of white spray tracing past *Rocky Ledge*. I didn't even realize it was my hydroplane. Jon was doing over 40 mph—so fast that most of the time the boat was riding on the engine's cavitation plate, the hull not even touching the water.

For my mother this was the last straw. She ran out onto the pier and frantically waved her arms at Jon as he came by on his second pass. By the time Sherry and I reached Sheep Island twenty minutes later the 15 was back on the skiff and my hydroplane was floating at the dock without a motor. I asked Jon what had happened. "I put the 15 on the hydroplane, but Mom made me take it off," he replied. "What was it like?" I asked, hoping for a direct infusion of excitement. "It was pretty fast," he answered. He was being circumspect because Mom was within earshot. Later, he told me the whole story.

During the last week of summer my father came up from DC to help close up the cottage. One sunny day he and my mother took the skiff with the 15 up to Cundys Harbor for lunch. I never thought to mention that the old engine had one serious quirk. The mechanism that prevents the engine from starting unless it is in neutral was broken when we bought it. When my parents came back down to the dock after eating lunch, my father made three mistakes. First, he untied from the dock before starting the motor. Second, he failed to make sure the engine was in neutral before pulling the starter. And third, he did not check the position of the throttle. There was another thing, too. The old 5-1/2 could be started while sitting down, but the big 15 had greater compression and required a lot more muscle. Even a strong man would have to stand up and put some weight into pulling the starter cord to get the thing going.

The reader can probably imagine what happened next. It was just lucky my father was not killed. He was, of course, thrown over the back the boat when the engine burst to life in forward at nearly full throttle. Without anyone at the tiller the boat then raced around in circles until my mother, overcoming her extreme terror, managed to climb back and take control of it. Luckily, the skiff did not collide with any other boats in the crowded harbor. A local lobsterman, muttering under his breath about the summer people from away, was able to help my father out of the water. I imagine that lobsterman entertained his buddies for weeks with the story.

We left Maine a few days later. I knew my mother's attitude about both my hydroplane and the old 15 had eroded from simple distrust to pure revulsion. She was now convinced, probably rightly, that the hydroplane was a life-threatening and reckless indulgence, and she made no secret of the fact that she hated the 15. It was too big, too loud, too hard for her to start when Jon wasn't around to drive it for her, and too damn dangerous!

The school year of 1963 went slowly by and I thought the whole thing had been forgotten. But my mother had already made plans. When we got to Maine in June the first thing she did was trade in the old 15 for a brand new 9.5 hp Evinrude. The smaller motor was reliable and easy to start, and had enough power to move the skiff along at a reasonable and safe speed. It was undeniably the perfect motor for my mother. "But the 15 was mine and Jon's," I complained. "We paid for it with our own money and you didn't even ask us." "I'm not going to discuss it," she replied in the voice with which we did not argue. "You have the 5-1/2, and that's more than enough for that nasty little boat of yours."

I used the hydroplane for one more season, but the summer of 1964 was the last one of my childhood that I spent full time in Maine. When I went back for a few days in 1971 the hydroplane was lying upside down in the woods next to *Rocky Ledge*. Paint was

The new hydroplane under construction in the author's garage.

peeling off and it was starting to rot. I didn't even try to get it into the water. The next time I got back to Sheep Island several years later the hydroplane was gone. I never did give it a name. But in the summer of 2018, I came across a set of original plans online and engaged a group of grand nephews and nieces in building a replica of the original. The legacy lives on!

The new hydroplane ready to launch.

CHAPTER 16:
Sea Fever

My mother's birth family was a large one. She was the eldest of seven children, and when she and her siblings were grown and married with children of their own, we counted 27 first cousins, many of whom I had never even met. On top of that were the extended families of my mother's cousins, among whom one was my clear favorite: "Cousin Alex" Haughwout, his wife, Ruth, and their four children, my second cousins Pixie, Peter, Pam & Penny. They lived on Byram Shore Road just outside Greenwich, Connecticut. Across the street was a small beach on Long Island Sound, and in back was about 100 feet of waterfront on the Bryam River. Cousin Alex was an adventurous man whose successful air conditioning business in Port Chester, New York afforded him the resources to own some impressive boats and recreational equipment, and to design and build his house and property to accommodate them.

The house was a 1-1/2 story affair he had built of cinderblock with large double pane picture windows in front overlooking Long Island Sound. Double pane insulated windows were not yet standard fare, and Alex, always an innovator, had fashioned his by hand. However, he neglected to properly seal the edges, and it was not long before condensation and dust built up between the panes, blurring the otherwise spectacular views. The southwest end of the attic, accessible only from a stairway outside the kitchen door, was his workshop, filled with all manner of tools and smelling of paint and fiberglass. In the backyard he had created a winter storage "harbor" for his sailboat by excavating a large grotto with a channel that opened to the Byram River. *Sea Fever*, a 1961 Mercer 44, rigged as a cutter with a 50' mast, was almost as big as his house and towered over it when the tide was high.

Cousin Alex's home was a wonderful place to visit, and my siblings and I were closer to his children, than we were to most of our first cousins. This was due, in large part, to the relationship between Alex and my mother, for they had grown up together and shared a close bond. "Kissing cousins" was how my mother once characterized it in a rare moment of candor. She always spoke highly and with great affection about "Cousin Alex". We often stopped by on our way up to Maine, or on the way home to Washington. Even better, however, Alex and his family often sailed up to Maine in the summer where we could all spend a few days together. The age range of my second cousins was not an ideal fit for me, since I was two years younger than Peter and two years older than Pam. Penny, the youngest, was about five years my junior, while Pixie was five years my senior. But that did not keep me from falling madly in love with Pixie when they sailed to Maine in 1963.

A year later, when *Sea Fever* stopped by for another visit, I joined the family aboard for an overnight cruise to Monhegan Island. I had never been there before, since none of our boats in those years were capable of traversing 30 miles of open water. But *Sea Fever* was more than up to the task, and we had a lot of fun exploring the island and seeing the rusting wreck of the D.T. Sheridan at Lobster Cove, still recognizable before it deteriorated to its current state. The harbor at Monhegan is not well protected, and that evening a strong south wind kicked up 6' swells that came barreling through the mooring field making sleep nearly impossible. The next morning we left Monhegan early under power on a southwesterly course, traversing diagonally across the heavy seas. Without the stabilizing influence of the sails, *Sea Fever* pitched, rocked, and rolled so violently that within a few minutes nearly everyone on board was sea sick. My pathetic and absurd appeals to "Stop the boat!" only elicited laughter from Alex, who remained immune to the malady that was plaguing the rest of us. Fortunately, by the time we got about halfway back to Sheep Island our course changed enough that we could raise sails, steady the boat, and get some hot breakfast into our stomachs. The misery of sea sickness was quickly forgotten.

My unrequited love for Pixie was reignited each time *Sea Fever* showed up in Maine, and it became more intense the summer Cousin Alex invited me to cruise with the family from Byram Shore to Casco Bay. That trip, in the summer of 1965, was memorable for several reasons. Our first stop was Block Island just off the north end of Long Island, New York. The place was still quite primitive in those days. That evening we went ashore to watch a movie in a theater that had only bench seats with no backs. Incandescent bulbs hanging from the ceiling and shaded with perforated tin cans provided the theater lights. The real reason for stopping at Block Island, however, was to join a racing regatta from there to Newport Harbor the next day. There was quite a large fleet of yachts involved, and although, much to our delight, *Sea Fever* was first across the finish line, we lost on handicap to a slower boat. Nonetheless, once we were at anchor Captain Alex mixed up a large batch of daquiris, a celebratory "sailor's drink", he told us, made with generous portions of rum. No one was monitoring my consumption, and several glasses later I passed out on a bunk below decks. I was 15.

Continuing north from Newport, we went through the Cape Cod Canal, then across a long stretch of the Gulf of Maine, mostly at night. I was assigned lookout duty for a good part of the evening, instructed to watch for logs and other navigation hazards, and also to keep alert for freighters and ocean liners heading in or out of Boston, since our course took us directly across a busy shipping lane. Alone on the bowsprit in the cold and dark I wondered what good I could possibly do regarding the first part of my assignment. We were motoring along at about 6 knots and I could see only a few feet ahead of me. I would not possibly have time to warn the helmsman if we were about to run into something. But I did enjoy the brilliant, sparkling phosphorescence we stirred up as we charged through the waves, as well as a school of porpoises that cruised along with us for several miles just off our starboard bow.

After my shift was over I gratefully retired to my bunk, where I slept soundly until first light. When I came back on deck we were in a thick fog. Alex asked me if I knew how to use a radio direction finder. I did not. He gave a perfunctory explanation, handed me a piece of equipment about the size of shoebox, square with a large dial on the top, and sent me to the bow to locate the signal from Halfway Rock. Somewhat lacking in confidence, and fully aware of what danger we could be in if my readings were inaccurate, I set the direction finder on the foredeck and did my best to get a signal. Miraculously, I was successful, and we were able to give Halfway Rock, still shrouded in fog, a wide margin to our port. Two hours later, with the fog finally lifting and the sun shining warmly, we pulled up in front of *Rocky Ledge*.

Sadly, Cousin Alex and his family could stay only a day or two, and I was not going to be continuing with them for the trip home. Early in the morning of the third day, before most of my family were awake, Alex hauled up anchor and *Sea Fever* headed south under power towards the open waters of Casco Bay. I was awake, and as soon as I saw them leaving, I threw on some clothes and raced to the south end of Sheep Island so I could wave goodbye as they passed. I don't think I have ever felt more forlorn and lonely than watching *Sea Fever*, brightly illuminated by the rising sun, as she grew smaller and smaller, then finally disappeared from view past Rogue Island.

I loved the Haughwout family perhaps even more than my own. Cousin Alex's wife, Ruth, was in my eyes the most beautiful woman in the world. She looked to me like a Greek goddess, was an amazing cook, and exuded motherly kindness in a way that, sadly, I did not often experience at home. Cousin Alex, himself, seemed to accept and respect me as his own son, often including me or assigning grown-up tasks that challenged my strength, abilities, and intelligence. I shared great affection with all four of their children, and as much as I loved being in Maine, I would much rather have been aboard *Sea Fever* with all of them.

My dreams seemed to be coming true two years later when, just after graduating from high school, Alex invited me to take a summer job working in the sheet metal fabrication shop of his air-conditioning business. I would be living with the family and earning $2.38 per hour, which in the summer of 1967 was pretty good money for someone with zero experience. I really enjoyed the work. The geometry involved in figuring out how to create complex ductwork fittings from a single flat piece of sheet metal was really challenging. I also enjoyed the company of the other 10 or so employees. We generally worked in teams of two to three men, doing both the manufacturing and installation of the ductwork. The older men were happy to give me a lot of instruction and guidance on the use of the heavy shop equipment, which included "brakes" for bending 8' and 12' sheets of galvanized steel, welding and cutting machines, and a large variety of hand tools. I was often paired with two fairly rough guys in their late twenties who both smoked constantly and would often wolf-whistle and make lewd comments at female pedestrians as we drove past in one of the company trucks. Generally, in addition to learning about working with sheet metal, my association with them was a series of lessons in how not to act in decent society.

The best part of the summer was that I was invited to sail with the family for their annual August cruise aboard *Sea Fever*. This year, instead of sailing north to Maine, we would be sailing south through the Intracoastal Waterway to Cape Hatteras, then back north along the Atlantic seaboard. Coming with us for part of the cruise would be Tom Riedel, Alex's shop manager, as well Pixie's best friend, Georgia. Alex's son, Peter, would also be joining us for part of the trip once we reached the Chesapeake Bay. What I did not know was that Alex was hoping Tom and Pixie would get along, for he was quite fond of Tom and saw him not only as the likely future owner of his business, but also as a prospective son-in-law. When I figured this out I began a campaign to sabotage any chance for such an outcome, mostly by inserting myself into any activity that might result in Pixie and Tom being alone together. The satisfying result was that Tom fell in love with Georgia, instead of Pixie. As of this writing they are still happily married.

As we sailed south from Greenwich, we entered the harrowing East River where five knots of tidal current swept us past Roosevelt Island and Hell Gate and the south end of Manhattan. We then passed the Statue of Liberty at some distance, sailed under the Verrazano Narrows Bridge, rounded Sandy Hook, and proceeded south along the coast of New Jersey. We found a sheltered anchorage for our first night near Fisherman's Cove inside the mouth of the Manasquan River.

Continuing south the next morning we anchored off Chincoteague Island, where Pixie, Georgia and I swam ashore hoping to see some of the famous horses. Instead, about 100 feet into the sandy terrain we started kicking up swarms of horseflies, which immediately attacked us. In a panic we raced back to the beach, dove into the waves and swam as far as we could underwater to get away. When we came up to grab a breath of air, swarms of flies still pursued us. Reaching *Sea Fever*, Alex had us haul up the anchor and we sailed away. Only when we were far from shore did we leave those tormenting little devils behind us.

Sailing into the Chesapeake Bay we stopped by Tangier Island, largely isolated since being settled in the 17th century. The people there still spoke with a thick accent derived from their English ancestral past. When we went ashore a couple of local boys in their early 20s immediately took an interest in Pixie and invited her to "go driving." I was about to intervene, but she wisely turned down their offer. There was nowhere to drive on Tangier, for the place is only a little more than a mile long. Nonetheless, a number of cars had been brought from the mainland over the years, most of which were broken down and left to rust wherever they had given up the ghost. Leaving Tangier we sailed through a field of crabs mating on the surface. Alex retrieved a crab net up from below and we set about catching dinner.

That evening, we pulled into a tiny town on Maryland's eastern shore—I think it was Crisfield—where Alex's son, Peter, joined us. After our crab supper Peter and I took a walk, for which I brought along a bottle of Apricot Brandy that I had won as a door prize at an air-conditioning industry convention in Port Chester to which Alex had sent me earlier in the summer. I was 17, but looked a lot younger, and the gentleman

The author aboard Sea Fever, ready to catch crabs in Chesapeake Bay. (Photo courtesy of Ruth Haughwout)

who handed me the door prize hesitated for a moment until I took it out of his hands, said thank you, and quickly sidled past. One of the first things Peter and I encountered as we strolled about the waterfront was a rustic movie theater with a prominently displayed sign indicating that the main theater was reserved for whites, while seating for "colored" was in the balcony. I was shocked that such overt racism could still be on display in 1967, but I was clearly out of touch with the culture in out-of-the way places like Maryland's Eastern Shore and the rural South.

Peter and I eventually found a spot to sit on a stone wall over the harbor where we delved into the Apricot Brandy. We were having a fine time of it until I knocked the bottle over and it shattered on the stone sidewalk. Back aboard *Sea Fever* I pulled out my guitar—I never went anywhere without it—and, in an exercise of poor judgement, serenaded Pixie on the forward deck with the Beatles' "Michelle" and other love songs while her parents were

The author serenades the Haughwout women aboard Sea Fever. From L to R: Penny, Ruth, the author, Pam & Pixie. (Photo courtesy of Ruth Haughwout)

trying to sleep in the forward berth just below us.

A few days later we sailed through Pimlico Sound and out the Wallace Channel south of Cape Hatteras into the North Atlantic. Within a few miles we crossed from the slate gray Atlantic into the crystal blue waters of the Gulf Stream, then turned north and headed towards home. My attentions to Pixie had been grating on Alex, and as the final leg of our trip progressed, his manner toward me became increasingly irritated. Finally, somewhere along the New Jersey coast, he called me back to the cockpit from the foredeck where I had been sitting with Pixie, and gave me a such a tongue lashing that I seriously considered jumping overboard and swimming to shore.

But it turned out that Alex needed me. *Sea Fever* was a big boat. She weighed 27,000 pounds and carried nearly 900 square feet of sail. The way she was rigged back then it was impossible to sail her without at least two strong crew members, in addition to the helmsman, to tend to the sails. Since Alex's son, Peter, was with us for only a couple of days during the two weeks of cruising, I was his replacement. I was still seething with anger and shame at being publicly berated in front of the family, but as we entered New York Harbor I had to spring into action tending the sails. My value as a crew member thus restored, the storm of emotions gradually faded and we ended our cruise on a high note, flying the spinnaker as we charged up Long Island Sound with a strong south wind behind us. That fall I started college and my days of carefree summer vacations were at an end.

Alex eventually sold *Sea Fever* to someone who took her to the west coast where we lost track of her. A few years ago, I was talking about boats with one of my neighbors in Bath when he mentioned that his father lived on a sailboat in San Francisco Bay. Questioning him further I learned that the boat was 44' long, then that it was a Mercer, and finally that it was named *Sea Fever*! As of this writing she is for sale again, and I keep thinking how nice it would be to have her back in the family.

Rocky Ledge, January 1992.

CHAPTER 17:
Return to Maine

Throughout the 1980s and 1990s I was living first in Los Angeles, then New Mexico, and had few occasions to get to the East Coast. In January, 1992, however, I was able to make a short trip to Maine. Until that time I had never been in Maine during the winter and had always longed to see what it would be like on Sheep Island. My childhood friend, Rob Miller, moved to Cundys Harbor shortly after college and had been building and renovating houses for a living. By chance, his work boat was in the water and he agreed to take me out to the island. It was frigid on the New Meadows River, and the shore around Sheep Island was caked in snow and ice. *Rocky Ledge*, tucked into a thick forest of snow-capped spruce, looked forlorn with its winter shutters up and the front porch bare of furniture. I had a camera along to commemorate my visit. The print I later sent to Alex was given a prominent place on his kitchen wall, both as a conversation starter for friends and family, and as a constant reminder of how much we both loved the place.

Finally, in 1996, for the first time in over 30 years, I was able to spend most of the summer in Maine. While there I made a point to visit all the people and places that had played a part in my childhood, both to rekindle fond relationships and to verify my recollections of these stories. I was pleased to find many things exactly as I had remembered them. Our log cabin in the woods of Brightwater was nearly unchanged in 30 years, and as I walked down the path to the water, every rock, tree, and shrub seemed so familiar that I walked part of the way with my eyes closed, just to see

The author, age 5, in the woods at Brightwater.

how good my memory was. Halfway down the path I got down on my hands and knees and examined the lichens clinging to the rocks, just as I had done at the age of six. They were beautiful: miniature ecosystems with an amazing variety of forms and colors. Down near our dock the forest of spruce and birch retained the same primitive feel that I had fallen in love with as a child.

I stopped for a few moments where four piles of loose stone marked the spot where my mother had wanted to build a cabin in the early '50's, before my parents discovered *Rocky Ledge*. My mother died of cancer in 1973. Although only 61, she had lived a rich life, full of music and art and the raising of five children. She had held deep attachments to her family, her church and her ancestral heritage. There were many places she might have been buried, each of which would have been appropriate. But her dying wish was to be cremated and to have her ashes spread in the New Meadows River between the two places in the world she loved the best: Brightwater and Sheep Island. As I continued down to the dock I knew my own dying wish would be the same.

Some things had changed for the better. I was happy to find that many forms of wildlife that were rare in the 1960's had made a comeback. Most notable were the birds of prey. When I was a child, I never saw an eagle, and could remember only one pair of ospreys. They had a nest in the exposed rigging of a sunken fishing boat in Sebasco. Now, however, I counted several pairs on Brightwater alone. And early one morning, as I was rowing through the Narrows, I spotted a bald eagle on the limb of a dead spruce tree. I shipped my oars and drifted along, watching him in silent fascination. A splash in the water behind me startled us both, and he spread his wings and flew off.

I turned to see a strange creature struggling in the water only twenty yards from me. It kept surfacing and disappearing, and seemed to have a combination of brown fur and silvery scales. I sat still as my boat drifted closer. The next time it surfaced I chuckled to myself. It was just a seal. But he had caught a huge fish, a striped bass nearly three feet long. As I watched, the seal attempted to eat his catch, unperturbed by my presence. He was trying to hold the fish between his flippers so that he could get a good bite, but it kept slipping out of his ungainly grip. It was a comic performance. Occasionally he would look up at me with curious, saucer-wide eyes, as if to inquire whether I was enjoying the show. We drifted along together for several minutes until, frightened by a lobster boat on its early rounds, the seal exited underwater with his prey.

The next morning, I came down to the dock at first light to go for another row to the Basin. As I leaned down to untie the painter there was a commotion in the seaweed at the water's edge ten feet in front of me. Something was thrashing around just below the surface. I watched in amazement. It was a mink, dragging a lobster by the tail up onto the shore. The lobster was putting up a huge fight, locking its claws onto the seaweed and thrashing its tail. The mink was only slightly larger than the lobster, but she was determined. She managed to pull the lobster free of its grip and up to the next rock. It was an awkward maneuver, for she was forced to move backwards, dragging the lobster only a few inches at a time.

Just then she looked up and saw me. Startled, she momentarily dropped the lobster, which immediately clamped down on another bunch of seaweed. The mink was confused. I could see that she was trying to decide between her hard-fought meal and her instinct to flee. My legs were now aching from squatting, but I stayed still, and the mink quickly decided that the threat I posed was not worth losing her breakfast. Again, she took the lobster's tail in her teeth and tried to pull it loose from the seaweed. After 20 or 30 seconds of furious yanking and struggling she succeeded, dragging her unhappy victim several feet further from the water's edge.

Finally, I had to stand up to relieve my aching legs. The mink, alarmed, dropped her prey once again. Once again the lobster clamped down on the seaweed. The mink looked back and forth between me and the lobster and once again, deciding that I was not as important as her meal, resumed her struggle. Within a few minutes she had managed to back her way up over the rocks and into the bushes, dragging the lobster with her.

I tiptoed up the ramp to the shore, climbed up to the woods and stood there quietly, hoping that the mink might cross the path. I was well rewarded. She appeared a few seconds later, dragging the lobster backwards down the path straight towards me. When she was only 18 inches from my shoes she turned, looked up and froze. Her shiny black eyes stared into mine. The lobster was still gripped in her teeth, and for a moment all three of us were still. Then, with a sudden burst of energy, the mink dodged sideways, disappearing with her prey into the blueberry and juniper bushes at the edge of the trail.

As I stood and listened to her rustling through the undergrowth, I wondered why I had never seen things like this as a child. Eagles, osprey, mink, sea bass—these were all recent arrivals, or perhaps re-arrivals. I realized that they were probably making a comeback after being nearly wiped out by DDT and other pesticides in the '40's and '50's. I thought of my two-year-old grandson, and felt glad that his childhood would be enriched by contact with wildlife that had not been available in my own youth.

Over on Sheep Island time seemed to have stood still, except that the trees seemed taller, now dwarfing the cottages.

Piglet in its final days as a planter.

Rocky Ledge looked the same, but there was no sign of *Betsy Boat*, which had rotted away years earlier. I found *Piglet* in the woods next to the porch. Poor *Piglet* was not in good shape. It had clearly suffered from years of neglect. But its sails and spars were still intact, wrapped up together and lying in the rafters of the cottage. I toyed with the idea of re-fitting it, but found myself overwhelmed with other repairs that needed to be made on the cottage.

Royal Tern, too, was in need of a great deal of work. The last time she had been in the water was in 1992. Since then she had stood, hauled up on the Brightwater shore, covered with a tarpaulin. Some of the pine strips near the keel had rotted and many of the nails and fasteners had rusted to the point that she would be unsafe in the water. Her sails and rigging also needed to be replaced. I went to visit her often, and longed to find the time and money to give her the attention I felt she deserved, dreaming of the time when I could sail her again.

Royal Tern in 2010 before its restoration.

The saddest part of my return to Maine was the loss of Christine Miller. The day I arrived I took the skiff up to Cundys Harbor and hurried up the pier to visit her at Holbrook's General Store. One of her daughters greeted me with the sad news that Christine had died just one week earlier. I was devastated, as was everyone else in the Harbor. Christine was deeply loved, and sorely missed. Her passing represented the end of an era for all who knew her.

But I did see other friends from my childhood. Rob Miller was now Chief of the Cundys Harbor Volunteer Fire Department. His two boys were busy gathering their own precious experiences: sailing, boating, building, and exploring on Sheep Island and the New Meadows River every summer. So too were new generations of the Showells, the Sargents, and our other neighbors on the island. Twelve years before, after not seeing or hearing from her in 20 years, I had located Sherry Adams and called her one January day to wish her happy birthday. The memory of our summers together was still alive, perhaps even enhanced by time, and we have remained good friends ever since.

Early in July I went to Sebasco to see what had become of Dutch Albertson. In front of his pier was a beautiful, turquoise-blue lobster boat that looked exactly like *Loa Lea*. But it bore the name *Sara C*. I tied up to the dock, where a teenage boy was fishing, and asked if Dutch Albertson still lived here. He looked me over quizzically and said, "My great-grandfather is up in the garage fixing the lawn-mower." I felt elated as I walked hastily up the pier to the garage. I called out, "Dutch?" A voice answered from inside the kitchen. "Ayuh?, come on in."

I opened the door and found Dutch sitting at the kitchen table. He was 89 years old and still going strong. I reminded him

Sara C, a nearly exact replacement of Dutch Albertson's Loa Lea, at her dock in Sebasco Harbor.

who I was, referring to the incidents with *Royal Tern* and *Piglet*, which he remembered clearly and with the same nostalgic fondness I felt. We talked about boats for a long time, especially Charley Gomes' boats. Charley had built *Loa Lea* in 1932, and Dutch swore it was the best lobster boat Charley ever built. The lines and balance were so perfect, he said, that even with substantially more weight and less power than some of the other big boats on Casco Bay, it consistently outran the competition at the annual Potts Harbor Lobster boat races.

In the 1970's after a problem with rotting timber in the transom and an unsuccessful attempt to preserve the hull with fiberglass, Dutch had commissioned the building of *Sara C* on exactly the same lines and proportions as Charley Gomes' earlier masterpiece. Dutch defied modern convention and had insisted

Sara C be made of wood instead of fiberglass. "I didn't want a damn Clorox bottle," he told me emphatically. "I wanted a boat just like *Loa Lea*." He got it, too. And a wall full of trophies in his den gave testimony to both boats' speed and dominance among the local lobstering fleet.

I asked Dutch what had happened to *Loa Lea*. "After we got all her lines and measurements," he said, "I took her apart piece by piece, brought her up to the back yard here and burned her. I couldn't just let her rot. She was the best boat I ever had."

Throughout the rest of the summer I continued to see *Sara C* making her rounds on the New Meadows River. And every time I saw her I felt a strange sense of pride, as if she really belonged to me, somehow. Or perhaps I belonged to her, as I belonged to the granite shores and spruce forests of the New Meadows River. For that summer had made me realize how much my spirit was shaped and honed by my love and attachment to this place, and by my childhood experiences on the coastal waters of Maine.

CHAPTER 18:
Melody Enters Our Lives

In 1996 our experience of vacations in Maine took on a new and much appreciated aspect with the use and eventual acquisition of a 27' Bristol sloop owned by my uncle, Peter Haughwout, who had purchased her in 1978 when he moved to Maine. *Melody* was a fine boat, and a radical step up from *Royal Tern*, which, as an open cockpit 21' daysailer, had a very limited range. *Melody* was a fast boat, outfitted with large sails, a roller-reefing jib, and a spinnaker. She also had a cabin that could sleep four, a small galley (kitchenette), portable head (toilet), and an engine well mounted with a 15 hp long shaft Nissan outboard. Uncle Peter had taken her on many week-long cruises up and down the coast of Maine. But by 1996 he was ready to part with her and all the hassles and expense of maintaining, insuring, and storing her. Without sufficient means to actually buy the boat at the time, I made Uncle Peter an offer: I would cover all the launching and maintenance costs, as well as the insurance, if he would let me use *Melody* for the summer. He agreed to this arrangement on the condition that he be allowed to take the boat for one week during August for his annual coastal cruise.

Thus, after a lifetime of sailing within only a few miles of Sheep Island, we could now take longer trips that included overnights. My brother Alex and I, in Maine together that summer for the first time in many years, wasted no time in testing our wings with *Melody*. At 1:30 in the afternoon on August 14, 1996 we set sail from our cove at Brightwater, heading for Monhegan Island, some 30 miles to the east in the Gulf of Maine. On board with Alex and me were

Melody on the New Meadows with the author at the helm. (Photo courtesy of Paul Rice)

his son, James (age 16), my "stepson" Alexander from a previous relationship (age 10), and my fiancée, Johannah, who is now my wife. Our relationship then was quite new, for we had met only a few months earlier when she was managing an art gallery in Taos, New Mexico that was exhibiting my watercolors. This was her first trip to Maine, her first time sailing, and the first time meeting my family.

Our larder was minimally stocked with some dishes that Johannah had prepared, a few snacks, and quite a bit of beer. Also on board was a treasure that Brother Alex discovered in a small book

Chapter 18: Melody Enters Our Lives

rack above a bunk in the main cabin: a large hard-bound volume bearing the title "Yacht Log Book and Guest Register Radio Log". The first six pages bore a few chicken scratches of data from Uncle Peter's first cruise in July 1979 with two of his siblings, my uncles John and Robert. There was a notation in pencil with an arrow to a slightly wrinkled and discolored spot on page 6 that read "John spilled drink at 4:10 pm". Other than that, the yacht log was completely empty.

Alex decided that we should follow Uncle Peter's lead and document our first trip aboard *Melody*. He began a running commentary that set a style that has lasted to this day, documenting our family's summer vacations in Maine. Alex would make note of the time, then write in sparse, abbreviated phrases with minimal or no punctuation:

1:30	Blachly Cove B'wtr
7:15	Well past Seguin turned on engine
7:50	saw seal 3 mi SSE of Pumpkin Is
8:00	gorgeous sunset 1.5 hrs W of Monhegan
8:10	saw 4 sec + 10 sec lights
8:12	lost 'em. Must have been a boat
9:10	ran out of gas. Refilled from spare tank. Difficult in dark.
10:00	moored at public mooring at Monhegan
10:30	sent Jamie and Alexander in rowboat to find matches
11:05	mackerel start jumping at garbage recently dumped (from hotel?)
11:43	lights out

Note: Excellent potato salad prepared by Johannah, eaten by all, even Jamie and Alexander, who don't like potato salad. Also, matches used to light Coleman stove to heat soup for dinner.

A little translation and explanation might make these entries a bit more meaningful to the casual reader. As noted, *Melody* was a fast boat, easily capable of 6—7 knots (7—8 mph) in a modest wind. Thus, the 30-mile trip to Monhegan Island should have taken 5 or 6 hours. But Alex's second entry, nearly six hours after departing from Brightwater, was made just after passing Seguin Island, not even halfway to our destination. In other words, there was almost no wind. Turning on the engine on a sailboat was tantamount to sacrilege among my family, which explains why we waited so long. It is also worth noting that we had no particular training in navigation, and without the benefit of modern GPS devices, we were dependent upon an old Coast Guard chart of the area. Navigation buoys with signal lights set to flash at various intervals were absolutely essential when sailing in the dark, and a great deal of our mental energy after the sun went down was consumed in searching, mostly in vain, for a flashing light that might provide some sense of where we were. It was little more than dumb luck that we found our way to Monhegan Island under these conditions, and that we were able to find a mooring in the small and unprotected harbor there.

The next day, after an early morning of exploring the island and finding that the one pizza joint would not be serving until noon, we decided that it would be a good idea to head for home. We were almost out of gas and would be dependent on the wind for most or all of our return trip. But we needn't have been concerned. The wind was blowing briskly from the north as we left the mooring, sailing almost due west on a close reach, *Melody* charged through the sea at near hull speed.

Alex continued documenting our progress:

Thursday 8/15/96

    7:30 am   *Associate capt'n Peter awakens sleeping hogs, ending loud snoring*

    7:50 am   *Breakfast at Monhegan House Café, where we all illegally used the upstairs bathrooms.*

NOTE: Blue aluminum skiff pulled up on beach + tied to anchor chain with 6" links.

Alex delighted in calling me "associate captain", pulling rank as the older brother, even though I was the one in charge of the boat. During this trip he came up with a variety of phony ranks, bestowing cumbersome and sarcastically flattering titles on each of us. The blue skiff mentioned here was a very leaky and nearly useless aluminum boat that we towed as our dinghy. It required frequent bailing.

Alex writes:

> *12:33 Jamie bails blue boat and notes that riding behind gives an interesting perspective on fast speed of towing boat.*
>
> *12:34 Hon. Associate Co-Captain Peter thanks official Blue Boat Bailer Jamie.*
>
> *12:37 Decision to drag Molson's Export Ail [sic] to cool them off*

There is an adage among sailors that the definition of "sailing" is long periods of boredom punctuated by moments of complete panic. In the long and uneventful sail back from Monhegan Island, boredom was offset by the consumption of beer, which inspired Alex to make increasingly inane observations about each member of the crew. Many comments were made about young Alexander, whose mother, unbeknownst to me, had given him $200 for the trip to Maine, a significant portion of which he spent on candy, soft drinks, and snacks until I took charge of the remaining money. The two cans of Mountain Dew he consumed in the first hour of our sail left him both hyper—which was not much fun to be around—and needing to pee every 10 or 15 minutes, which under windy conditions was also more than a little challenging.

Gradually the wind shifted further to the east, so we raised the spinnaker and gained a little more speed. Other than having to bail our leaky skiff every 45 minutes or so—a task made moderately exciting by the speed at which we were sailing—our trip home was mostly uneventful. We passed the time by tending the spinnaker, drinking too much beer, placing 1¢ bets on how long it would take to reach various navigational buoys and other waymarks, and making snide comments about any other sailboat we saw in the distance, fully confident that *Melody* was the most beautiful boat on the ocean.

As we rounded Small Point into the New Meadows River the wind shifted again and we had to take down the spinnaker. We crossed our fingers as we entered the Bear Island strait, encountering a strong outgoing tide and headwind from the north. The wind increased the further we went up river, and we made it back to our mooring at Brightwater without once having to start the engine. It had taken us a little over six hours to cover the 30 miles from Monhegan Island. We were ecstatic, and now so completely enamored of *Melody* that we soon purchased her from Uncle Peter.

Melody under sail. Watercolor by the author.

Not only was *Melody* now a cornerstone of our summer adventures; the log book, too, had become an important part of our lives, documenting nearly every visit by family members and their guests. When we ran out of pages fifteen years later, I purchased another, so we have a nearly continuous record of our family's Maine vacations spanning the last 30 years.

CHAPTER 19:
Crossing in Fog

One August evening several years later, my brother Alex and I, together again in Maine, were late getting back to Brightwater from town and found ourselves facing a moonless night as we started down the long, wooded path to our dock so we could get across to Sheep Island. Even after a lifetime of traversing that path we stumbled along. My flashlight's batteries were dying and the light was barely enough to illuminate tendrils of mist moving ghostlike through the trees. It was a disconcerting sight, and as we reached the shore for the one-mile boat ride across to our island cottage, our worst fears were realized: it was a "pea soup" fog on a dark night, and we had no compass to guide us.

Nonetheless, I felt that I could guide our skiff safely across. I had decades of experience in these waters and was sure I was intimately familiar with every shoreline and reef. That night there was rich phosphorescence, and the water sparkled brightly wherever it was disturbed by an oar or a propellor. I told Alex with great confidence that I could watch the wake behind our boat, glistening like the Milky Way, to ensure that our course, once set, was maintained straight across the river.

As Alex and I got into the boat, a 1965 13' Boston Whaler, we found too late that every surface was dripping wet from the fog. The seats of our pants were immediately soaked through. It did not seem like an auspicious start, but we were anxious to get back to our cottage where we could warm up in front of the wood stove. The aging outboard started on the second pull and ran smoothly: a good sign. So, we cast off from the dock and motored slowly along the shore, headed for Davis Point, where we could then set a course across the river. The night was so dark and the fog so thick that we had to stay within a few feet of the shore to avoid losing our way.

As we rounded Davis Point we took a southerly turn of about 15 degrees that would put us due west toward Sheep Island. If we could just reach the other side of the river, even off course, we could then feel our way along the shore and reach the island. We set out into the darkness, untethered from the visual world. It was so dark that we could not even see the lobster buoys that thickly dotted this part of the river. I drove along slowly to avoid damaging the boat or motor should we hit one. But at this slow speed it was hard to judge whether the wake behind us was actually straight. I noted that the only real danger we faced was the unlikely possibility that we would get so far off course that we could end up going south, out to the open waters of Casco Bay. In the blinding darkness I could not get that thought out of my mind, so I adjusted our course ever so slightly to the right, just to be safe. Then we hit a lobster buoy and the engine stalled.

By the time I got the line disentangled from the propellor and the engine running again, all sense of direction had evaporated. Gone was the line of phosphorescence that had guided us to this point, and gone was my confidence. We peered about through the fog, hoping to see a glimmer of light from some cottage on the shore, but there was nothing. There was not even any wind by which we might gauge our direction. We were completely lost. I chose a course at random and we motored on slowly.

Puttering along at about three miles an hour made what would normally have been a five-minute crossing seem like an eternity. As the minutes ticked by, the damp air grew colder and the inky darkness grew ever more oppressive. Suddenly, there ahead of us appeared the vague silhouette of a tree-lined shore, eerily devoid of houses or any sign of civilization. "I think this must be the south end of Sheep Island," I said to Alex with some relief. "Let's just follow the shore," he replied, less convinced.

Unable to see any details in the gloom, we turned to the north and inched along, trying to keep within view of the shore without running aground. We were going so slowly that the old engine, unused to idling at low speed, threatened to quit. Our anxiety only mounted as we encountered an outcropping of rocks that should not have been there. It was obvious this could not possibly be Sheep Island. So where were we?

"I think this is Long Island," said Alex with some exasperation. Long Island, nearly a mile northeast of Sheep, had the only other uninhabited point of land on this section of the New Meadows. "I think you're right," I responded, shivering. "If we follow the shore to the south we can bear to the starboard when we reach the point and find our way to Dingley Island, and from there we should be able to follow the reefs to Sheep." He agreed that this was a good plan. I turned the boat around and tried to keep sight of shore as we headed south, but in the swirling fog all was lost in shadow. Squinting through the darkness I tried to maintain a course I thought was south. It wasn't.

After several minutes I guessed that we must have passed the end of Long Island so I began bearing right, as planned. Dingley Island is only a couple hundred yards from Long Island, so it should not have taken us long to reach it. But after several more minutes there was no sign of land. Anxiety crept back, and each minute that passed reinforced the gnawing fear in the pit of my stomach. We were hopelessly lost. Could we already be so far down river that we had passed Cundy's Harbor? Could we even now be in the open waters past Bear Island? There was no telling. Anything was possible in this darkness, and only pure luck could now guide us.

We motored slowly on, grateful at least that the old Nissan outboard was behaving itself and that we were in a seaworthy boat. Boston Whalers are famous for being unsinkable. Print ads from the 1960's would show a boat that had been sawed in half at midships, with one man driving the engine on the back half and another happily rowing away in the front half. It was an impressive visual. At least we were not in danger of drowning.

Suddenly, after about twenty minutes, looming ahead and on both sides of us emerged the fog-shrouded forms of several small boats. We had wandered into the middle of a mooring field. I cut the engine, squinting through the darkness, trying to determine just exactly what boats these were. My flashlight, now almost useless, provided a feeble ray of light that fell upon a sailboat I recognized with alarm. We were back on the Phippsburg side of the river, exactly opposite from where I thought we would be! Alex and I marveled at how utterly wrong we could be; how totally disorienting it was to be blinded by the fog. Now that we knew where we were, however, we could set a reasonably accurate course for home—just as long as we could keep the boat going in a straight line.

But we had already learned that following a straight line in the dark in a small boat with an outboard motor and no compass is not so easy. I decided to drive at top speed—lobster buoys be damned. At least it would take only few minutes to get across, and our wake would be brightly lit from the phosphorescence and might provide some directional guidance as originally hoped. But it was nerve-wracking, and at this speed the fog settled thickly on my glasses, adding to the feeling of being completely blind. After a few minutes, thinking we must soon be reaching the other shore, I cut the engine back to a crawl and mopped the fog from my glasses. It was just in time. The motor scraped bottom, and there ahead of us, lying low and dark, was the ominous form of a seaweed-covered reef. I cut the engine entirely and tilted it, and in the eerie silence we paddled closer, hoping to see something we could identify.

As we neared the reef the boat touched bottom and we could go no further. But through the fog, which breathlessly faded in and out, we could see the faintest silhouette of a shoreline with trees. If it was, as we now dared to hope, the southern point of Dingley Island, all we had to do was follow the reefs along to the south. Sheep Island would be only a few hundred yards away. But it was still guesswork, and we might just as well have come upon the reefs at Cundys Harbor, a mile to the south. We dislodged ourselves from the mud, and once in deep enough water I lowered the engine and started her up again.

Unfortunately, the old Nissan was a deep shaft motor on a boat designed for a short one, so we needed to be in over two feet of water to run it. That put us far enough out that our view of the shore and our sense of direction were lost yet again. By now, Alex and I were feeling quite humbled. We were also quite cold and wet and more than ready for this adventure to be over. I thought our best chance would be to stay in shallow water, if we could, using an oar to test our depth as we inched along. At least we would be close to shore that way.

We ran aground several times over the next few minutes, which was both unsettling and reassuring. But we were making progress. Luckily for us, the tide was low enough that the reefs were partially exposed as we came upon them, working our way to the south. Halfway between Dingley and Sheep there is one reef that juts out further to the east than the others. When we thought we had reached it we had to leave the shallows and venture out into the river again. I tried to gauge our direction and distance, and made a turn to the right when I thought we were far enough past the reef. But we were enveloped in darkness, and by now my flashlight's batteries were completely dead.

After a few more minutes, ahead of us and to the left I thought I saw a glimmer of light. I cut the engine and called out. Marilyn Breed, one of our neighbors on Sheep Island, responded. She had heard our engine and our voices through the stillness of the night, and for several minutes had been waving a lantern from her dock. Marilyn was an amazing woman, still occupying the summer cottage on Sheep Island that her grandfather had built in 1908. She was older than me by about 20 years, but endowed with a fun-loving and youthful spirit, and was uncowed by social norms. In her late seventies at the time, she was adventurous, highly educated, fiercely independent, and a strong athlete. Earlier that summer she had amazed everyone by swimming across the New Meadows

River—a very cold swim of nearly a mile—without the benefit of a wet suit. Marilyn was also competent in the many skills required for island living, such as handling boats and motors, tying knots, chopping firewood, and dealing with heavy propane tanks.

Following the light from Marilyn's lantern we motored slowly into the cove, wending our way between half a dozen boats on their moorings. Marilyn greeted us

"Blachly Point in a Fog" Watercolor by the author's father, 1934.

warmly and peppered us with some rather pointed questions about what we had been doing on the river in such conditions. We gave a quick overview of our adventure and expressed our heartfelt gratitude for her help. Then, shivering and wet, we ventured the final 75 yards to our own dock.

Back in our cottage, as we warmed ourselves with a glass of wine in front of a roaring fire, Alex and I congratulated each other on a successful crossing. But we both knew congratulations were not exactly in order. We had experienced one of the more terrifying and dangerous conditions that a boater can encounter on the coast of Maine, and our success was far more a matter of luck than of skill. "Just think," reflected Alex, "What could have happened if the tide had been full, or if there had been a strong wind and rough sea, or if Marilyn had not been there to guide us in that last 100 yards, or if the old Nissan had decided to give up the ghost in the middle of the river!"

CHAPTER 20:
Passings

In the summer of 2004, while we were living in Vermont, Johannah arranged for her mother, Nell, to come for a visit, along with her sister, Linda, and Linda's teenage daughter, Alison. None of them had ever been to Maine and they were all entranced when we took them there, especially Nell. Her life-long dream had been to live in a simple log cabin. So intense was this longing that she had altered an old cardboard-backed poster of a snow-capped mountain we found in her attic by drawing in a little cabin near the summit, with smoke spiraling from the chimney. She immediately fell in love with the rustic simplicity of the *Field Cabin*, and her sense of wonder upon first arriving at Sheep Island was captured in one of Johannah's photographs.

We often managed to get the family out on the water while they were here, and with the mid-summer weather being mild and perfect it was hard to tell which they liked better between the exhilaration of sailing and the thrill of speed in the Boston Whaler.

Johannah was trained as a photo journalist, but her real passion, in addition to music and literature, was creative photography, especially fashion and still life. Before we met she had worked for a time with Matthew Ralston doing high-end fashion photography in Los Angeles and New York. For her own private work, she had a large collection of vintage and unusual clothes and accessories in which she liked to dress her subjects—usually, a willing friend or relative—and have them pose under her direction. She especially liked working with young people in this context, and they were

Johannah's mother, Nell, arriving at Sheep Island for the first time. (Photo by Johannah Harkness)

usually thrilled to be a part of her creative adventures.

Out on Sheep Island, although having no access to her costumes and wardrobes, she did find a very unusual chair that had been built from driftwood by someone who had rented *Rocky Ledge* for a few weeks several years earlier. The chair was more like a throne and was vaguely suggestive of maritime mythology, as if one might find King Neptune lounging in it. Duly inspired, Johannah recruited her niece, Alison, as a model and set

Johannah's niece, Alison, as a Sea Nymph. (Photo by Johannah Harkness)

Crossing the new Meadows from L to R: Johannah, Linda, Alison, Nell.

up an outdoor photo shoot on the rocks in front of *Rocky Ledge*. Undaunted by lack of access to her abundant costumes, she improvised using the materials at hand, most of which included seaweed, driftwood, sea shells, old lobstering gear, and dried starfish. Alison, thus dressed in a rather skimpy costume of found items, took her seat in King Neptune's throne and struck a wide range of poses while Johannah's camera clicked away. I had been asked to go do something else during this time so as to afford privacy to Alison. But reviewing the photos later I pointed out to Johannah that Alison had attracted the attention of some local lobstermen, whose boat can be seen getting ever closer in many of the photographs.

Alison was a very slender young woman, a fact that played into another of Johannah's creative ventures. Long a critic of traditional gender roles, and inspired by the large array of cooking and cleaning utensils packed into the kitchen at *Rocky Ledge*, Johannah recruited Alison to serve as a second pair of arms while she herself posed as a "Kitchen Goddess" in the style of Saraswati, Durga, Kali, and other multi-armed Hindu goddesses. After setting up the shot, Johannah had me snap the shutter as she and Alison assumed various poses. With Alison's body completely hidden behind Johannah, the effect of the second pair of arms is both natural-looking and rather disconcerting, while the social statement of the resulting photograph is clear enough.

In April, 2011, as soon as Johannah and I purchased our first home in Bath, we had Nell, who was in failing health, come to

Johannah, with extra arms provided by Alison, posing as the Kitchen Goddess.

live with us. Nell was delighted to be in Maine, and as the weather warmed towards summer we took her often to Brightwater and Sheep Island. She would have been happy to spend the rest of her days in the *Field Cabin*, but that was not to be.

Nell in the Field Cabin. (Photo by Johannah Harkness)

Chapter 20: Passings

Less than a year after joining us Nell took a turn for the worse. She was a tiny woman, not even 90 pounds, and she was losing weight. We took her to the hospital where she seemed to revive a bit. I spent the afternoon with her listening to hits from the 40s and 50s—mostly Frank Sinatra tunes to which she sang along. That evening she was unable to sleep and one of the nurses applied a fentanyl patch, which knocked her out so hard that she was still asleep when we arrived the next morning. Unable to rouse her, and upon learning of the fentanyl we convinced the head nurse to revive her with a shot of adrenaline. Mercifully, this worked, and feeling much better Nell said she wanted to come back home with us. The hospital required that she be transported in an ambulance, so we had the driver follow us home.

It was a beautiful early spring day in March. The forsythia bushes along our driveway were blooming, and birds were fluttering about and chirping as we wheeled Nell's stretcher up the steep stairs from the street to our front door. The driver was amazed to find where we lived, for he had roomed there some 30 years earlier while in high school, back when the house was owned by Olive Palmer, a kindly English teacher who provided a safe home away from home for many of her students. We took all these as good signs, and once Nell was settled into bed with unseasonably warm spring air drifting through her open window, Johannah took her leave to go do some shopping. After sitting quietly with Nell for half an hour I left her to nap while I did some work at the back of the house.

I was still at work when Johannah, back from her shopping, came running out to get me. "Something has happened to Nell!" she exclaimed. We returned to Nell's room to find her unresponsive, her eyes rolled up, and her breathing labored. "I'm sorry," I said to Johannah, "She is on her way home." It was a severe shock to Johannah. Blinded by her hope, she fully expected her mother to be with us for several more years. We stayed up all that night with Nell, holding her hand and singing softly to her some of the old gospel hymns she loved. By mid-morning the following day, with

Johannah and me at her side, she took her last breath. The next day, with a small group of friends, we held a short bedside memorial service for her, then accompanied her body to be cremated. In June, Johannah's sister came up from Texas, and the three of us took the whaler out to the middle of the New Meadows and held a simple burial at sea, mixing some of Nell's ashes with some from Johannah's father, Bill, which she had been keeping since his death twelve years earlier.

Nell's passing was the beginning of a cascade of losses. The following year, emphysema caught up with my uncle Peter Haughwout, from whom we had purchased *Melody* nearly two decades earlier. Johannah and I were with him on his last night, taking shifts at his side along with his wife, Marianne. For the last few days of his life he was put on hospice, and when the time came to start giving him morphine to ease his breathing I consulted with him. "Peter," I said, "I guess you know that once we start the morphine it's pretty much a one-way trip." He nodded. "Is that what you want?" I asked. Again, his only reply was to nod. A few hours later Johannah and I had just collapsed on the living room couch after a late-night shift when Marianne came out and told us that Peter was gone. He was the youngest and last surviving of my mother's six siblings, and had long been one of my favorite relatives. Peter had stipulated that his body be donated to science, so it wasn't until

The author's uncle, Peter Haughwout, at the helm of Melody.

a few years later that Marianne received the cremated remains. Fulfilling Peter's final wishes, Johannah and I took Marianne out near Flag Island in *Melody*, where we spread his ashes into the sea. It was a bright sunny day with a light breeze and we were all amazed at the glitter reflected back to us as Peter's ashes sank into the cold, clear waters of Casco Bay.

The following spring, Johannah's beloved kitty, Gracie, passed away at the age of 18. Gracie and her sister, Kate, had been with us from the day they were born in 1997. That year, Johannah had told me she wanted a kitten for her birthday, but three successive trips to the local animal shelter in Taos, New Mexico had yielded nothing. I was told by the staff to come back in the spring. Finally, unable to provide Johannah a surprise kitten on her birthday, I presented her instead with a watercolor of a Siberian tiger cub that I had completed the night before. Johannah was gracious in her appreciation for my efforts, but she wanted a real, live kitten. When I told her the only cat at the shelter was a pregnant mama she said "Let's go get her!" So we did. The mama cat was so heavy with her babies that we thought she would give birth on the way home. But it was a couple more weeks before the kittens came, and during the long wait the mama cat spent most of her time lying down with Johannah's warm hand on her expansive belly. Finally, she gave birth to four darling babies, two of which we kept.

Johannah was devasted by the loss of Gracie, and insisted that we give her a proper cremation. We couldn't do it at home in Bath, but one of my cousins—whose affection for animals far exceeded any feelings for his fellow humans—generously offered to provide transportation in his workboat out to Sheep Island, as it was only March and I had no boats yet in the water. As I was constructing the pyre from a quantity of dried firewood we had brought with us, my island neighbor Rob Miller showed up with a flask of something with which to commemorate the occasion and to warm us against the cold March air. He was skeptical of my efforts, for he had tried quite unsuccessfully to cremate a large dog several years previously. But he did not know that I had witnessed many cremations in India, and he changed his opinion as I put the finishing touches on Gracie's well-constructed funeral pyre. Two hours later, with the pyre reduced to smoldering embers, Johannah collected some of the ashes as a keepsake, leaving the rest to wash away with the high tide.

Toward the close of 2015 we had three more losses: my oldest brother, Jim, and sister, Brett in successive months (as noted earlier), and just one month later, Johannah's brother, Marc. The string of losses finally reached a crescendo in 2016 when Gracie's litter mate, Kate, passed away the same night that my father died in August, followed by his sister, my Aunt Daphne, in December.

A feeling of loneliness descended upon us as we entered the cold and dark of winter. There was no replacing those so dear to us whom we had lost. But a little more than two years later we adopted a pair of feral rescue cats in time for Johannah's birthday in February 2019, just before the Covid Pandemic took root. Forced suddenly into social isolation we took as much comfort in our cats as they took in having a secure and loving home after the travails of the animal shelter. We also developed even greater appreciation for the fresh sea air of the New Meadows River and the woods of Brightwater and Sheep Island where activities with friends did not come with the attendant concerns of catching a deadly air-borne disease that was keeping us so isolated while indoors.

CHAPTER 21:
Home at Last & More Adventures

Johannah and I moved to Portland, Maine in 2008, and on April 1, 2011, which would have been my mother's 100th birthday, we moved into an aging house we bought in Bath, just 12 minutes' drive from Brightwater. Since that time my family and I have done much to improve and preserve both the *Field Cabin* and *Rocky Ledge* for future generations. In 2009 my father, who was very happy with our progress in bringing the family back together and managing the Maine properties, commissioned the restoration of the *Royal Tern*.

Royal Tern under sail in 2012 after her restoration.

The author with his brother, Alex (on the left), on a joyride across the New Meadows River, 2018.

The following summer, on June 21, 2010, my brother Alex, joined me for a commemorative 50th anniversary sail to Halfway Rock. We did not take *Piglet*, whose seams had long since come apart—she was serving as a flower planter at *Rocky Ledge*. Instead, we sailed in *Melody*. We were joined by Alex's son, James, whom we sent ashore at Halfway Rock in a small kayak to retrieve another stone or two to join the "original" that Alex and I had brought back to Sheep Island 50 years earlier. Those two stones from Halfway Rock now maintain an honored spot, side by side in the cottage at *Rocky Ledge*.

Eight years later, on June 24, 2016 about 2:00 in the afternoon, I had just left the *Field Cabin* on Brightwater, headed back to Bath, when my phone rang. It was my cousin, whose family owned the cottage next to ours on Sheep Island. "Where are you right now?" he demanded with an uncustomary sense of urgency. "I just left Brightwater headed to Bath," I responded. "Well, you better turn around. Sheep Island is on fire!" "I'm on my way," I said, and hung

Chapter 21: Home at Last & More Adventures

Sheep Island on fire, June 24, 2016.

up. Five minutes later I was in my family's 13' Boston Whaler, headed at full speed across the New Meadows River. There was a strong wind from the southwest, and clouds of heavy smoke were rising from the center of the island directly behind *Rocky Ledge*, blowing towards the northeast.

A microburst during the "Patriot's Day Storm" in 2011 had leveled about five acres in the thickest part of the island's forest. Although some of the downed trees had been cleared away, most were left in a tangled mass of softwood limbs and branches that died and quickly dried out. We knew it was a tinderbox, but there was little we could do about it. As I drew closer to the island, flames were visible through the trees close behind Rob Miller's house. I had barely tied up when crews of firefighters started arriving, first from Cundys Harbor, then from adjoining towns and communities.

Soon, two Maine Forest Service helicopters arrived and started dumping 500-gallon loads of water on the fire's northern and eastern peripheries, pulling fresh water from the pond on Dingley Island just to our north. My niece, Jenny, and her three children were staying at *Rocky Ledge* at the time. They had already jumped into action, removing precious family heirlooms, family photos, and mementos from the cottage and carrying them down to the pier while trying to stay clear of the dozens of volunteer firefighters who were arriving and setting up gasoline-powered pumps and transporting equipment and hoses up to the shore. Despite the efforts of the Forest Service helicopters and the scores of volunteer firefighters now assembled on Sheep Island from nine different municipalities, the fire continued to spread. The wind would sometimes send burning embers 100 yards or more, starting new blazes outside the main fire. I tried to be useful by fetching cans of gas from Cundys Harbor to keep the pumps running, and by ferrying firefighters back and forth as needed. Our dock, which jutted out quite far into the river, turned into a primary staging area, and several pumps were set up there and on our front rocks, as well as in the cove around to our north. But many of the pumps were not powerful enough to send seawater up the slope towards the center of the island where it was needed, so the heavy lifting had to be done by the two helicopters.

Without the help of two Maine Forest Service helicopters dropping dozens of 500-gallon loads of water on the raging fire, every cottage on Sheep Island would have burned.

Incredibly, despite the wind and nearly impossible conditions, the fire crews managed to contain the blaze within about 3 hours. Not a single cottage was damaged, though flames came within 10 or 20 feet of a couple of them. After the flames had been doused there was still a great deal of work to be done dealing with hot spots.

Volunteer crews, joined by Rob Miller and his sons, continued working all night and for the next two days, cutting a perimeter firebreak around the burned area and extinguishing smoldering tree roots and hot spots in the loamy soil, which at any time could erupt back into flames.

Dozens of volunteer firefighters from 9 nearby municipalities worked tirelessly for up to 72 hours to quell the flames, clear a firebreak, and extinguish hotspots.

Over the years, many of us on the island had complained about having to pay taxes for island properties that had no municipal services, but no one voiced such concerns after the fire! The response from the area fire services, including the Maine Forest Service, was beyond anything we might have imagined, and every family on the island owed the survival of their cottage to the hard work of the volunteers.

Later that summer, a group of neighbors from both sides of the river met with a representative of the Maine Forest Service to learn about the national "Firewise Community" program, which offers resources and advice about ways to protect homes located in high-risk areas in the event of a wildfire. As of this writing Brightwater, Wynburg, and the adjoining Wynburg East communities are participating in the program.

One June day in 2017 I was cruising around the Kennebec in my skiff when, on the far shore opposite our home I came across an attractive cabin cruiser at its mooring. Admiring its fine lines as I motored slowly past I noticed a postcard-sized hand-written note pasted to one the cabin windows. I doubled back and read "For

Sale. 1971 Grand Banks 32' Sedan. $20,000. For more information call (207) 443-XXXX." Intrigued, I took a photo of it and called as soon as I got home. The next day I met with the owner and got a tour of the interior, and immediately fell in love the boat. $20,000 was a lot of money, and I knew that the yearly maintenance would not be cheap, but my wife, seeing how smitten I was, encouraged me to go ahead and buy the boat, using what remained of the small inheritance my father had left me.

Gracie III at the author's dock on the Kennebec River in Bath.

The next day I was the proud owner of a yacht that could literally cruise the entire eastern seaboard and beyond. But I could not take delivery until I got my own dock and mooring organized, so for a few days my "new", 46-year-old Grand Banks 32' Sedan would have to stay on its former owner's mooring across the river. A day or two later I took my young grand-nephew, Leo, for a tour of the Kennebec, ostensibly looking for nautical treasures that might have washed up on the shore. In the early summer all sorts of things can be found, such as detached mooring balls, wooden oars, life-jackets, docking fenders, and the like. As we motored past the Grand Banks I nonchalantly asked, "What do you think of this thing?" "Wow," replied Leo, "I can't imagine a Blachly ever owning a boat like that!" I didn't tell him I had already bought it. Two days later, when he stopped by and saw the very same boat tied to the dock in front of my house, his exclamations of total surprise were most satisfying. Even more was his utter delight when I took him for a short jaunt down the river to see one of the new Zumwalt Class Destroyers at the Bath Iron Works and let him steer the boat most of the way. Leo immediately declared himself my first mate.

The author with his grand-nephew, Leo, at the helm of Gracie III.

Thus opened a new chapter in my family's maritime adventures. The best part for me was that Johannah, who was not fond of sailing, was much happier in the Grand Banks with its spacious cabin and smooth ride. Powered by a single Ford-Lehman 120 hp diesel engine, the boat was quite slow, and at 17,000 pounds it plowed through the seas without the kind of pounding we had endured for decades with our smaller boats. The first time I took Johannah out in it we were cruising down the Kennebec when I turned and asked what she thought. "I LOVE it!" she exclaimed. I had planned to name the boat *Grace*, but named her *Gracie III* instead. The first Gracie was Johannah's beloved cat, who had lived with us for 18 years. The second was Johannah's niece, who had also lived with us for a year when she a teenager.

The first time I tried to land at my dock I discovered that with a single inboard engine and a full length keel, a boat will not respond well to the rudder when backing. "Put her in forward to get her pointing where you want," the previous owner told me, "Then throw her in reverse." Seventeen thousand pounds of boat has a lot of momentum, but I learned quickly enough how to bring it into a dock, even when the tide was running a couple of knots. It had only one significant mechanical problem: one of the pipes in the internal cooling system was leaking, a fact I only discovered on July 4 as I was maneuvering for a mooring between a fleet of smaller boats on the Bath waterfront to watch the famous fireworks. Just as I was pulling up to a vacant mooring, pushing against a strong outgoing tide, the engine overheated and quit. With no backup source of propulsion we were at risk of being swept down the river. I took a chance and restarted the engine, gunning it in forward just enough that one of my guests on board was able to snag the mooring line before it quit again. It took three people to pull *Gracie III* against the swift current and get the line secured.

Johannah with Gracie, 2014.

We were mighty lucky, but now I was in a real fix. I had a boat full of guests and was a mile downstream from my own mooring with a motor that would not go more than a few hundred yards before overheating; and it was getting dark. Fortunately, several officers from the Bath Police Department were cruising around in their launch and came within earshot. They hesitated when I asked them to take me to shore, but quickly obliged when I explained my dilemma. I made my way through the thick crowd that was gathering on shore and managed to hitch a ride back to my house from a friendly stranger who was driving along the waterfront looking for a parking spot. I then retrieved my 13' Boston Whaler and raced back down river to join my guests. The Whaler, with its 25 hp outboard, had plenty of power and, after enjoying the fireworks, we were able to push the Grand Banks back up river to my mooring with one of my guests at the helm, since I was too low in the water driving the whaler to see where we were going.

The next day I looked for a piece of pipe that could replace the one that had failed, but the only thing I could find at the local hardware store with the right dimensions was a section of heavy-duty vacuum hose. I did not know that the vacuum hose, though extremely strong, would not respond well when heated to near boiling. Three days later, with some of the same guests on board, we took a short cruise a mile up and across the river to Days Ferry, where the engine again overheated and quit, this time with an incoming tide. A quick inspection revealed that the vacuum hose had become distorted from the heat and one end had slipped off its fitting. Fortunately, I had a couple of gallons of engine coolant on board, and after refastening the hose as best I could and refilling the radiator, we were able to limp home slowly, reaching my dock just as the hose failed a third time. The next day I purchased a ten-foot length of 1-1/2" copper pipe at a local plumbing supply wholesaler and fashioned a replacement part that permanently solved the problem.

No longer trusting that my beautiful old boat was 100% trustworthy, I made a practice of towing my skiff with its outboard whenever we went out. I also purchased a membership with Sea Tow in case we ever got in real trouble. With these safeguards in

Gracie III on her mooring at Brightwater, 2019.

place, I felt enough confidence to take Johannah for an overnight cruise to Monhegan Island in late July. Our course would take us through Boothbay Harbor by way of the Sasanoa River, which connects the Kennebec just below Bath to the Sheepscot River. I had ventured part of the way down the Sasanoa a week or two before, but got cold feet as I approached "Upper Hellgate", a narrow passage where the tidal current rushes through at 6 or 7 knots. "Cold feet" is a bit of an understatement. I was scared, in fact, for I could hear and see the rapids in front of me and did not know at that time if the channel was deep enough, or if I would even be able to get back up river against the current.

If I had been in my skiff I would have chanced it, for a small, lightweight boat with an outboard motor is highly maneuverable, and even running aground would not be too much of a concern. Not so, however, with a 32' wooden boat that weighs nearly 9 tons. There was not even enough room in the channel above Hell Gate to make a u-turn, so I had to make a rather desperate five-point turn instead, alternately jamming the boat into forward and reverse to get turned around while the swift current dragged me ever closer to the point of no return. I was mighty relieved when my boat was finally headed back upstream away from danger! Later, I consulted with a neighbor who was familiar with the local waters, and he reassured me that the channel through Upper Hell Gate was quite deep, and that I would have no problem. However, he did advise against trying to go against the current in such a slow boat. I rescheduled our 30-mile trip to Monhegan Island, therefore, on a day when we could catch an outgoing tide in the morning and arrive at our destination before dark.

The trip was fabulous and cemented our love of *Gracie III*. The dining table in the main cabin easily converted to a berth that could be combined with the seating around it to create a small but comfortable bed, just wide enough for the two of us. We greatly preferred this to the forward cabin, which was quite a bit smaller, with less headroom, and much more subject to the motion of the boat in any kind of sea. This was an important consideration since the harbor at Monhegan Island is not well protected from the prevailing southerly winds, and rarely offers a calm anchorage. Having departed from Bath early in the morning, we reached Monhegan shortly after noon and were able to hike around the island and enjoy an excellent meal at the Island Inn before retiring to our boat for the evening.

The next morning, I awoke just as the sky was starting to lighten in the east. Since we had to be back in Bath that afternoon I decided to depart right away and cruise by Eastern Egg Rock on the way home to see if there were any Puffins still nesting there. While Johannah snoozed comfortably, I got the engine going, cast off the mooring, and eased *Gracie III* through the channel between Monhegan and Manana Island. As we headed north on a calm sea I sipped on a hot cup of freshly brewed coffee. Such on-board comforts had been previously unknown to us, and our appreciation for *Gracie III* continued to grow.

Arriving at Eastern Egg Rock in mid-morning, we tied up to a mooring on the north side and were delighted to see that the place was alive with large numbers of nesting puffins and black guillemots. We watched from *Gracie III*'s rear deck, eating a hot breakfast while volunteers from the Audobon Society, which manages the island as a bird sanctuary, moved about to various viewing stations among the rocks. Puffins and guillemots were flying all around us like little airborne torpedoes, diving into the sea and sometimes coming up with two or three small fish in their bills. It was thrilling. On the way back to the Kennebec River in time to catch the incoming tide, we came across a giant ocean sunfish flopping about at the surface. It was at least 6' long, and looked for all the world like the severed head of a much, much larger fish. I wondered if it was in distress, but learned later that these huge fish often warm themselves this way in the sunlight at the surface. They are also reputed to be quite comfortable, even friendly around humans.

Later in the summer we took friends out to Seguin Island, 2-1/2 miles off Popham Beach at the mouth of the Kennebec. There are several public moorings available in the north-facing cove at Seguin, and though there is no dock, one can land a dinghy on the small beach if the waves are not too high. Seguin is a wonderful place to visit. The original lighthouse was commissioned by George Washington in 1795. The current lighthouse was built in 1857 and is now maintained by the non-profit Friends of Seguin Island. Volunteers give tours to visitors, allowing them to climb the stairs and access the walkway at the top of the lighthouse. On a clear day one can see Monhegan Island to the east, Portland to the southwest, and even Mount Washington to the northwest. As long as we owned *Gracie III* we made trips out to Seguin at least once every summer, bringing friends and relatives—especially younger ones who could romp around the island and experience the thrill of climbing to the top of Maine's second oldest lighthouse.

I had a special duty in mind for *Gracie III* in September 2017, the first year I owned her. My father had died in August the year before, and I had set September 21 of 2017—which would have been his 100th birthday—as the time for a family gathering to commemorate his life and spread his ashes in the New Meadows River, as he had instructed me. *Gracie III* was large enough to accommodate all 19 family members who participated. But we faced a challenge getting the boat around to the New Meadows from my dock on the Bath waterfront, for there was a tropical storm churning just off Cape Cod. It had hardly moved in 3 days, generating huge waves throughout the Gulf of Maine.

The author's younger daughter, Sathari, with her grandfather in 2015, age 97.

Finally, if my father's ceremony was going to take place, I would have to brave the seas and bring *Gracie III* down the Kennebec, around Point Small, and up the New Meadows River to Brightwater. My younger daughter was with me for the six-hour trip. Coming down the placid waters of the Kennebec River gave us no hint of what we were about to face. But when we got past Fort Popham at the mouth of the river the incoming waves were reaching heights of 12 or 13 feet. I had never been in seas like that and did not know how *Gracie III* would perform. But I needn't have worried. She had no trouble at all, and though it was both exciting and uncomfortable, we never felt unsafe, even as we made our way through the treacherous passage at Point Small, where spectacularly breaking surf would give any yachtsman pause.

At the end of that first season I contracted to keep the boat in the water at DiMillo's Marina in Portland. Because the aging hull was made of wood, I did not want to haul her out to be stored on land, for the wood would inevitably shrink as it dried. Seams would open up, and the boat might leak so much when put back in the water that she could sink. At DiMillo's the boat would be safely behind a seawall and would have shore power, so I could keep the cabin warm with a portable radiator and keep the batteries fully charged. Further, we would have access all winter to the marina's facilities, including heated bathrooms and showers. Johannah and I were looking forward to having *Gracie III* serve as a little home away from home. But we had not counted on the air quality inside the cabin declining so much once the door and the windows were closed. The smell of diesel fuel emanating from the bilge, which we never noticed during the summer, was a bit too strong for us, and we had to give up on the dream of having *Gracie III* as a winter weekend get-away.

In April 2018, as soon as the Kennebec was free of ice and I could get my dock and mooring in, I retrieved *Gracie III* from DiMillo's and brought her home, passing close to Halfway Rock along the way. I also started keeping an accurate log book, making note of departure and arrival times, engine hours, waypoints, fuel consumption, and any unusual sightings or occurrences. This proved enormously helpful, along with *Melody's* log book dating all the way back to 1996, when I applied for my Sea Captain's License from the US Coast Guard; for in addition to passing written exams in seamanship and navigation, every applicant for a professional captain's license needs to document at least 360 days at sea since the age of 16, including at least 90 within the three most recent years. With the log books I was easily able to prove that, and then some!

For the next five years *Gracie III* proved herself to be a truly fine boat, but logistical problems were arising that made my holding on to her quite challenging. One winter I kept her in the water at Robinhood Marina down the Sasanoa River from Bath. Marina staff moved her without telling me and in a severe winter storm one of the cleats on the dock broke free. Actually, a 3' plank to which the cleat was fastened pulled away. It had been held in place by only a few galvanized nails and should never have been used to secure a heavy yacht like *Gracie III*. Nonetheless—and despite the fact that my boat suffered more damage than the dock—the marina manager told me we wouldn't be welcome there the following season.

The next winter I went back to DiMillo's in Portland, but another winter storm caused a 4' tidal surge, allowing huge waves to overtop the seawall. *Gracie III* got badly battered. Two of the cleats on the rear deck pulled out and the swim platform got sheared off against the dock. Another Grand Banks in the adjoining slip rode out the storm without any damage, but once again I was told *Gracie III* was no longer welcome. The insurance company gave me a generous check for the damage, but cancelled my policy. Any loss or damage in the future would be entirely my responsibility.

Running out of options, and still unwilling to haul her out for the season, I arranged to keep her at the town dock in Wiscasset the following winter. It was critically important to have access to shore power to keep her batteries charged. If the bilge pumps failed for an extended period of time, even a slow leak could fill the bilge and do substantial damage to the engine and electronics below the cabin floor. Although *Gracie III*'s hull was remarkably tight for a 50-year-old wooden boat, she did have some minor leaks, enough to make me nervous about leaving her unattended for extended periods of time—and that winter Johannah and I were planning a trip to Portugal, our first overseas adventure in more than 20 years.

The harbor at Wiscasset is famous as a "hurricane hole" where ships had weathered the severest of storms for centuries, and the town dock did have shore power. Further, *Gracie III* would be sharing the dock with *Virginia* (a newly christened reproduction of the first English ship to be built in America in 1607), whose crew would be checking on her several times a week. Since I served as one of the designated volunteer captains for *Virginia*, other crew members were more than happy to keep an eye on *Gracie III*. The Harbormaster assured me that he would, too. But in the middle of January, while Johannah and I were enjoying sunny weather in the south of Portugal, the Harbormaster sent me photos he had taken in the middle of yet another severe winter storm. The tidal surge was

Gracie III at the town dock in Wiscasset in the midst of a severe winter storm, January 2024. A 4-foot tidal surge has put the entire pier under water.

so great that the pier was completely awash. The ramp to the dock had become dislodged at the shore end and the electricity was cut off. *Virginia* and *Gracie III both* looked in great peril.

To make things worse, Johannah and I contracted Covid at the tail end of our trip, and by the time we got home at the beginning of February I had determined it was time to sell *Gracie III*. As of this writing she has a new owner who loves her as I did. He has given her a new name, *Shanti*, and is upgrading some of her systems. She now has a new mooring in the middle of Damariscotta harbor. I still look at her longingly when I am up that way, but I am also keeping my eyes open for something a little newer and a little smaller that I can trailer and maintain on my own—for I don't think my adventures on the Coast of Maine are yet over.

Fred Blachly's great grandson, Leo learns to row. Watercolor by the author.

APPENDIX I:
Creating a Lasting Legacy

There are thousands of family vacation cottages and camps in the state of Maine that are now getting into their second, third, and fourth generation of ownership. Because of the way families grow or contract over time, the transition between generations is often fraught with problems. Too often, well-intentioned parents pass on a property to their children as "Tenants in Common." My father passed *Rocky Ledge* to me and my four siblings this way in 1985, and problems immediately arose. Each Tenant in Common has all the rights and privileges of ownership, but none of the individual responsibility. In other words, one sibling could occupy the property without contributing a dime to its maintenance, or make radical changes without consulting the others, or—in what may be a worst-case scenario—force a sale in order to cash out on their portion of the asset.

In 1985 my sister and her family were living in England and foresaw no prospect of coming to enjoy the place anytime soon, so she did not contribute anything to the maintenance. I was living in Los Angeles, struggling financially, and saw little prospect of being able to enjoy or contribute anything. My next older brother, Jon, did not have any interest at all in participating, and promptly turned his 1/5th share over to Alex, who was second oldest and spent more time in Maine than any of the other siblings.

But Alex was still in graduate school, working on his PhD and teaching as an adjunct professor at the University of Pennsylvania.

He was in no position to cover the property's expenses; nor was my oldest brother, Jim, who was living in Maryland at the time with his wife and four children. For several years, only Alex's and Jim's families were able to spend any time at all in Maine, with Jim contributing as he was able, which was not very much. My father did not want to be involved in his children's finances, and told me in the summer of 1996 that he was not planning on coming to Maine anymore, anyway. He did make one or two trips after that, but only to stay at the *Field Cabin*, and though he continued paying for most of the expenses related to the *Field Cabin* and the Brightwater Club, he had no involvement with *Rocky Ledge*. Alex, therefore, heroically covered nearly all the expenses for *Rocky Ledge* with little help from his siblings for more than a decade.

Johannah and I moved to Vermont in 2002 to attend graduate programs at Antioch University, and after living "out west" for 22 years I was finally able to get to Maine on a regular basis. In fact, I was so excited to be that close to Maine that I would drive the 4 hours from Brattleboro two to three weekends a month when the weather allowed. My own financial situation was finally starting to improve, as well, so I was able to begin contributing to the expenses. But the tensions between my older siblings had reached a crisis. In 2003, at the age of 86, my father made his last trip to Maine to attend his brother-in-law's funeral. He then formally turned over responsibility for the *Field Cabin* to his children.

Like thousands of other families that struggled with the disposition of inherited vacation properties in Maine, we would have to make some hard decisions. The most common approach to this problem, we discovered from consulting with a local lawyer, was for one family member to buy out the others. None of us liked this idea. I felt there might be a way to engage all the siblings and ensure that their children and future generations would not be excluded from being able to use the properties. I suggested that we create a family trust of some kind and develop a financial plan, a firm set of by-laws, and rules to govern everything from a calendar to the use of boats (not everyone in the family knew how to sail, or was familiar with the operation of outboard motors).

Alex agreed to give this approach a try, and with his two adult children, Margaret and James, we began creating a set of principles and guidelines for governance. It was an arduous and time-consuming process. We created a financial plan that included annual dues each voting member of the trust would pay—whether or not they made use of the cabin or the island cottage—and a fee schedule with a daily rate for dues-paying members and different rates for other categories of family members and guests. Throughout this process I was the liaison with my older siblings, keeping them informed and inviting them to share their thoughts and suggestions for by-laws and the whole concept of getting rid of the Tenants in Common mess by putting ownership of both properties into a legal entity of some kind, perhaps a trust, or LLC. It was critical that I gain their trust if they were ever going to relinquish their 1/5th shares of ownership. Otherwise, we would forever be under the threat that one of them or one of their heirs could force a sale.

The following year, on August 8, 2004, we held our first formal "annual" meeting at the *Field Cabin*, attended by Alex, Margaret, James, and myself. Among the items of business, we named our new organization the "Blachly Maine Trust." Every direct descendant of our parents would automatically become a member, subject to their abiding by the by-laws. But the decision-making body would be limited to seven "directors" with no more than two from any generation of any branch of the family. The four of us, as the founders of the "BMT" (as we called it then), would serve as directors, with me as President, Alex as Treasurer, and Margaret as Secretary. We agreed on a budget, which would include revenues from directors' "dues" of $400 each per year, as well as "usage fees" that would be paid by everyone who stayed at either *Rocky Ledge* or the *Field Cabin*. We also reviewed the condition of each property, the docks, and the boats and motors, and created a schedule of needed repairs along with assignments of who would undertake them. We then hammered out a framework for our bylaws. We felt we were off to a good start.

For the next five years we continued refining the by-laws and testing our cooperative operating agreement. It was working well. However, there was one sticking point in my view. The by-laws stipulated that if the "trust" was ever disbanded and the properties sold, the proceeds would be divided between the various directors "in good standing." I knew that this was going to be a problem for my two oldest siblings, and that they would never turn over their 1/5 ownership of *Rocky Ledge* under these conditions.

We finally agreed on a different approach, and in 2009 we formally changed the by-laws to stipulate that in the event the directors unanimously decided to sell the properties, all proceeds would be distributed to a non-profit charitable organization. This provision ensured that no family member would be tempted to "cash out." In the fall that year we filed incorporation papers with the State of Maine as "Blachly Maine Properties Association, Inc", a mutual benefit not-for-profit organization—not a tax-exempt charity, but like a neighborhood association.

There were several features about our new structure that made it work so well, in addition to those mentioned above. Creating a daily rate for the use of either property ensured that a large portion of our operating costs would be equitably distributed, based on how much time each family member spent there. Further, every family member, before making use of either property, would sign and return a copy of our guidelines, initialing each provision, to ensure that there could be no misunderstanding about what was and was not allowed.

We gave "directors"—who would be contributing to costs whether or not they used the properties—certain benefits, including a lower daily usage rate and the guarantee of at least one week of exclusive "alone time" each summer. Importantly, we also established a clear process by which any member could apply to become a director. They would have to show a committed interest by renting one of the places for at least a week on two consecutive summers, and they would have to agree in writing to every provision in our bylaws and guidelines. Acceptance of a new director would be by consensus of the existing directors, a provision intended to minimize the possibility of personal conflicts interfering with the orderly management and enjoyment of the properties. As of this writing, all "branches" of our family are represented by at least one director, with the exception of my brother, Jon, who has no children and continues to have no interest in our family properties, though as a "member" of the BMPA he is always welcome to use them.

In 2008, just as Johannah and I were moving to Portland, Maine, my father, now age 91, asked for help getting moved out of the DC apartment he and his wife, Helen, had inhabited for 35 years. Helen had suffered a couple of fractured vertebrae in two consecutive falls, and since she was not willing to let a physical therapist into her apartment, her doctor demanded that she go into rehab for a few weeks at a nearby retirement residence. My father went with her, and in less than two weeks they decided they preferred the conveniences there and were going to move in permanently. Of all the siblings, I was the only one who could make myself available, though I did get brother Jim to drive up from Georgia to assist for a week.

I was shocked at the early signs Jim was showing of Parkinson's Disease. Jim had joined the military in the mid-1960s, had attended Officer Candidate School, then risen to the rank of Captain and was awarded two medals for valor while serving consecutive tours of duty in Viet Nam. Unfortunately, he was exposed at least twice to Agent Orange, which the Army claimed was harmless. Decades later the Veterans' Administration finally acknowledged the causal connection between Agent Orange and Parkinson's Disease. By 2008, Jim's symptoms were becoming severe. He seemed incapable of making executive decisions, so I ended up giving him instructions, mostly telling him where to take the cart-loads of stuff we hauled out of the apartment.

Chapters could be written about Jim's and my efforts, but there were two important outcomes relevant to the Blachly Maine

Captain James Blachly at far right in Vietnam in 1967. At 6'6" he towered over most of his colleagues.

Properties Association. The first was the trust I built with Jim. He and I, the oldest and youngest siblings separated by almost exactly 8 years, had always been close. Besides being born on the 13th and 16th of November, respectively (eight years and three days apart), we both played guitar and had a love of traditional American music. When I was 12 he introduced me to the music of Ramblin' Jack Elliott, with whom I have had a life-long friendship, and he taught me some early finger-picking blues and bluegrass tunes. I still play one of the tunes he composed in 1965. Further, we both had mechanical skills. In fact, after leaving the Army Jim worked as a professional mechanic, specializing in the restoration of classic cars from the 1920's and 1930's. One of the cars he restored, a 1932 Packard Touring Car, is in the permanent collection of the Smithsonian Institution.

1932 Packard Touring Car

Jim had also helped me rebuild the big straight-eight engine of my 1939 Packard hearse when I was 15—a vehicle that horrified my mother and that she made me sell as soon as I got it running. Over the years since then Jim and I had worked together on many other vehicles, as well. While in DC together helping my father, I explained to Jim what we were trying to accomplish with the new family corporation, which we now called the "BMPA." He warmed to the concept as I told him that we were hoping his older son, Eric, would soon become one of the Directors.

The other development, which would have far-reaching beneficial consequences, was that I reconnected with my father and earned his complete trust by being there for him when no one else could. While I was still in DC after getting the furniture moved into his new apartment at the Georgetown Retirement Residence, Helen called and said she thought my father was having a heart attack. I raced the 12 blocks from his old apartment—arriving even before the medics—and helped the residential staff administer aspirin and amyl nitrate. My father was fully conscious, though in significant pain. The amyl nitrate gave him a horrendous headache, but he was alive! With Helen as a passenger, I followed his ambulance to the hospital.

The cardiologist explained that if my father were a younger man the obvious treatment would be to insert a stent, but that because of his advanced age, addressing the blockage in my father's right ventricle medicinally might be a more attractive and safer option. My father readily agreed. Left alone for a few minutes he turned to me and said, "Pete, if the worst should happen I want to be cremated and my ashes spread in the New Meadows River between Brightwater and Sheep Island." The significance of this was not lost on me. In August 1973 the family had gathered in Maine for the final disposition of my mother's remains. Before she died of cancer in January that year she had given exactly the same instructions that my father now gave me.

Fortunately, my father recovered, and a couple of days later I drove him home from the hospital. He was in high spirits. As we

Frederick Johnson Oatman Blachly, the author's father in 1960.

drove through the narrow streets of Georgetown he pointed out a house that had belonged to a former Navy Admiral whose daughter he had once dated. "Did I ever tell you about the time I met her sister, Patricia?" he asked me. I had heard most of his stories and jokes more than once, but I didn't know this one. "No," I said. "Well, she's one of only two women who would never speak to me again." Now my curiosity was piqued. "Her nickname was 'Tattie'. I was at their house one day when she walked in wearing a tight-fitting pink cashmere sweater with 'Tattie' embroidered across the left side. I asked her, 'What do you call the other one?'"

I nearly lost control of the car. My father was a master of puns and spontaneous one-liners, and the timing of his delivery was always perfect, as if he had practiced for months. "So, who was the other woman who would never speak to you again?" I asked. "I met one of my neighbors out walking her dog one day," he responded "and asked her the dog's name. She said 'Theophilus'. 'That's *the awfullest* name I ever heard,' I said. She would never even say 'hello' to me after that!"

My father was unusually effusive in expressing his appreciation for the timely assistance I was able to provide during the move and his ensuing health crisis. Even Helen thanked me, saying she did not know what she would have done without my help. A few days later my father put me in charge of his finances and medical care, introduced me to his CPA, and asked me to drive him and Helen to the lawyer's office where they both changed their wills, making me the executor of their estates and giving me power of attorney for their medical care.

When Helen died the following year, my father made a gift of her modest estate to his five children and made an additional gift to the BMPA that allowed us to make some significant improvements, including installing metal roofs on both the *Field Cabin* and *Rocky Ledge*, as well as putting in a full bathroom and laundry with septic system at the *Field Cabin*. This modernization was not undertaken lightly. Primitive living conditions were an important part of our experience of summers in Maine, and we were determined to keep *Rocky Ledge* off the grid while making the *Field Cabin* a little more convenient for aging family members and for those with young children.

By 2009 Alex, Margaret, James and I had been managing our two vacation properties cooperatively for five years as we refined our bylaws and rules. Things were going along smoothly, and we felt that we were ready to start including other family members. I had already been in conversations with two of my brother Jim's children, Eric and Jenny. Because Jenny's relationship with her parents at that time was on shaky ground they had agreed that Eric should apply to become a director, and that he would represent them both. Eric was then duly elected, and our board of directors expanded to five.

I was still deeply concerned about the ownership shares held by Jim and Brett, however. For years I had been keeping them both in the loop as we refined our bylaws, gradually building their trust in what we were trying to accomplish. Changing the provision in our bylaws about the disposition of the properties in the event that the BMPA was ever disbanded—directing that all proceeds would be given to a non-profit charitable organization instead of being divided among the directors—went a long way toward giving both of them confidence that our intentions could be trusted.

But time was ticking away and both Jim and Brett were in failing health. Finally, in late 2015 they both signed over their 1/5 ownership shares of *Rocky Ledge* to the Blachly Maine Properties Association. Brett died just weeks afterwards on October 22, succumbing to a decades-long battle with cancer, and Jim unexpectedly succumbed to pneumonia while in rehab for a fractured hip less than a month later. They were 72 and 74 respectively. Before my father died in August the following year, just three weeks before his 99th birthday, he made another gift to the BMPA to serve as a modest endowment, enough to ensure that even in times of financial difficulty we would be able to pay for taxes and insurance so that neither property would ever be lost or have to be sold. His legacy lives on, and the circle of his descendants and extended family who are able to enjoy the use of the properties continues to grow, now reaching into 5 generations.

APPENDIX II:
Bylaws of the Blachly Maine Properties Association, Inc.

Author's note: More than one lawyer has remarked that the BMPA bylaws are overly complex. Although that may well be true, they have served the family well for more than 20 years and have helped ensure that that the BMPA properties are maintained and that the uses and costs are equitably shared among the current four generations of the Blachly family. It is the author's hope that other families with shared vacation properties may find these bylaws helpful.

ARTICLE I: PURPOSE
Blachly Maine Properties Association, Inc. (hereafter, BMPA) is established to own and manage Blachly family properties in Maine for the mutual benefit of all the descendants of Elisabeth Macdonald Blachly and Frederick Johnson Oatman Blachly.

DEFINITIONS:
- *Board of Directors:* Group of BMPA Directors in good standing
- *Consensus:* all voting members are in agreement or have abstained with no opposition.
- *Director:* an individual who is in good standing within the BMPA organization and has voting rights
    - *Resigned director:* a former Director who has voluntarily terminated his/her directorship and voting rights.
    - *Revoked director:* a former Director whose directorship has been terminated by the Board of Directors and is not eligible to vote or rent either properties.

- o *Suspended d*irector: a Director who has voluntarily suspended his/her directorship but continues to incur fees and assessments. During the time of suspension, his/her directorship may not be filled nor can the suspended Director vote on BMPA decisions.
- *In good standing:* no outstanding financial obligations to the BMPA and not in violation of the rules and regulations as determined by the Board of Directors.
- *Major decision:* any decision by the BMPA that a) has a financial impact of $250 or more, b) substantially alters a BMPA owned property/asset that changes the appearance or functionality, c) will result in additional financial, special assessments or, d) affects an aspect of the property that may have emotional or historical significance to other family members.
- *Majority:* greater than 50% of voting members are in agreement.
- *Member:* any direct descendent of Elisabeth Macdonald Blachly and Frederick Johnson Oatman Blachly.
- *Reasonable notice:* communication to members and directors in a timely manner that allows awareness of an upcoming event or decision.

ARTICLE II: BMPA JURISDICTION

- The BMPA is the owner/manager of *Rocky Ledge* on Sheep Island, the owner of the *Field Cabin*, and the owner of other assets as listed in the "BMPA Handbook." Because of the structure of the Brightwater Club, two individual persons must be voting Directors for each Brightwater leasehold. The two individual voting Directors of the Brightwater Club for Lot 1 (the *Field Cabin*) represent the BMPA, not themselves. Other properties and assets may be added from time to time.

ARTICLE III: MEMBERSHIP

Every Descendant of Elisabeth Macdonald Blachly and Frederick Johnson Oatman Blachly shall automatically be granted membership in the BMPA. Membership privileges include the right to use any BMPA property subject to availability, fees, and other conditions as determined from time to time by the Directors, and to participate in meetings, committees, and discussions regarding BMPA business. Membership cannot be revoked, but the privileges of membership as outlined herein may be suspended or terminated for cause at the discretion of a ¾ vote of the Directors.

ARTICLE IV: DIRECTORS

The BMPA may have up to 7 Directors. BMPA Directors (hereafter, Directors) must be direct descendants of Elisabeth Macdonald Blachly and Frederick Johnson Oatman Blachly (EMB/FJOB). No more than two children of the same generational descendent may be Directors at the same time.

A) FINANCIAL RESPONSIBILITIES

In addition to any usage fees, each Director will pay quarterly base fees which are due July 15, October 15, January 15, and April 15. The amount of the quarterly fees is determined by a majority vote of the Directors. Additionally, special assessments may be required as determined by at least a ¾ vote of the Directors in good standing and are due at a time determined by the Board of Directors. Each Director is encouraged to make an anonymous annual individual contribution to the BMPA of not less than $10.00.

B) USAGE OF BMPA PROPTIES

Each Director in good standing is guaranteed up to one full week of private use of at least one of the BMPA properties each summer between June 1 and August 31 at the Directors' reduced daily rate, not including specific weeks as determined by the Directors. Until April 15 each year, Directors have first rights to reserve use of BMPA properties.

C) NEW BMPA DIRECTORS

Any direct descendant of EMB/FJOB may request to become a Director of the BMPA. Admission of an eligible candidate into the BMPA will be by consensus of the current Directors in good standing, provided that there exists a vacancy. Any descendant of EMB/FJOB who wishes to become a Director of the BMPA must:

i. Rent one or both of the BMPA properties for at least 4 (four) days in a season for 2 (two) consecutive years at the Relative rate, after which,
ii. submit his/her request for Directorship in writing to the Board of Directors. This request must include the following:
   a) a letter of intent that includes a specific agreement to abide by the By-Laws of the BMPA and to perpetuate its spirit;
   b) a copy of the BMPA by-laws with each provision initialed
   c) letters from 2 (two) existing BMPA Directors endorsing the application.
iii. A one-time application fee of $100.
iv. Attend at least one annual meeting either in person or by real-time electronic medium prior to being voted in.

D) TERMINATION OF DIRECTORSHIP

BMPA Directors may resign at any time or have their Directorship suspended or revoked for one of the reasons described below:

i. Expiration.

In the event of the death or legal incapacity of a Director, his/her Directorship in the BMPA expires. The descendant of a Director who has died or is legally incapacitated may, at his/her request, be placed at the top of the waiting list for admission as a Director. His/her admission to Directorship will not require an admittance fee.

ii. Resignation.

If a Director resigns, his/her descendant, at his/her request, will be placed at the top of the waiting list for admission as a new Director. Their admission to Directorship will not require an admittance fee. A resigned Directorship may be filled by the first qualified candidate at the next annual meeting, or at a special meeting called by the president. A director who has resigned from the BMPA may not vote but may rent either property at the Relative rate.

Reinstatement:
  a) Upon payment of all monies past due to the BMPA (quarterly dues, usage fees, and special assessments) that were in arrears at the time of resignation, a resigned Director may apply to be reinstated if a Directorship position is open and is voted upon by a consensus of the existing directors.
  b) No additional fee will be required when a resigned Director is reinstated.

iii. Revocation.
  A Director may have his/her Directorship revoked by a vote of at least 3/4 of the Board of Directors for behavior that the other Directors regard as a violation of the guiding principles of the BMPA. A Directorship revoked by vote of the Directors may be filled by the first person on the waiting list at the next annual meeting or at a special meeting called by the president. A revoked Director loses all privileges of membership to the BMPA, may not rent any property, and may not stay as a guest of another member or Director. A revoked Director has no right to reclaim any monies paid to the BMPA prior to the revocation.

  Reinstatement:
    a) A revoked director may reapply for a membership to the BMPA by ¾ vote directorship after a period of one year.
    b) A non-refundable fee of $100 will be required to reapply for membership.

ARTICLE V: OFFICERS
The BMPA will have four officers:
  1) A President, who facilitates the reservation calendar, runs meetings, and sets meeting agendas;
  2) A Vice-President, who acts as President when the President cannot serve;
  3) A Treasurer, who collects BMPA revenues, pays BMPA bills, and maintains all financial records;
  4. A Secretary, who records and distributes the minutes of all official meetings.

The term for officers shall be three years (starting in 2004). Every three years an election for all positions will be held at the annual meeting. By written request of two or more BMPA Directors, however, an early election for a new officer or new officers will be held at the next annual or special meeting, provided that the secretary has received the written request at least one month before the date of the meeting. There is no term limit for officers.

ARTICLE VI: MEETINGS

GOVERNANCE

The BMPA meetings will observe Robert's Rules of Order.

A. QUROM

For normal administrative purposes, a quorum will be considered met when at least 50% of the BMPA Directors in good standing are in attendance. However, all major decisions require the approval of at least 3/4 of the Directors represented either in person, by phone or other real-time electronic medium, or by written proxy relating to the specific item under discussion.

B. NOTICE

The President shall ensure that each Director is given reasonable notice of any meeting and of any major decision item to be considered at any meeting.

C. ANNUAL MEETING

The BMPA shall have an annual meeting at a time convenient to the BMPA Directors as determined by the President. The meeting will take place at a location and in a manner determined by the President. During the annual meeting, an overview of the state of the BMPA will be summarized (reports on financials, conditions of assets, improvements and needed repairs, and old and new business matters) and any other matter that the Directors shall deem relevant to the BMPA.

All meetings are open to all BMPA members, and all members of the BMPA are encouraged to attend meetings in person or by other communication methods. While only Directors can officially vote, all Members are encouraged to provide input.

E. OTHER MEETINGS

The president or any three officers may from time to time call other meetings of the Board of Directors as deemed necessary provided that reasonable notice is given to all Directors and for the purpose of making urgent decisions.

F. MINUTES

The Secretary shall ensure that minutes of each meeting are recorded, including the following information: Directors in attendance, proxies, and any decisions made. The Secretary shall also ensure that such minutes are distributed to all Directors in good standing within 30 days of the meeting. Directors shall have 30 days from receipt of the minutes to respond with any additions, corrections or concerns. Any disagreement about the content or meaning of any item in the minutes that cannot be resolved through informal discussions shall be resolved at the next annual meeting or conference call, and any action dictated by that item will be put on hold until it can be resolved. This caveat does not apply to items approved or rejected by vote of at least 3/4 of Directors.

G. PROXIES

A Director in good standing may appoint a proxy to represent him/her in all matters or in specified matters any other descendant of EMB/FJOB at any meeting of the Association. The appointment of any Proxy must be approved by unanimous consent of all other Directors in good standing in attendance prior to the start of the meeting. Such approval may be by electronic media.

ARTICLE VII: SPECIAL PROVISIONS

A. FISCAL YEAR

The BMPA's fiscal year will run from January 1 to December 31.

B. RESERVE FUND

The BMPA will maintain bank accounts and a reserve fund of an amount to be determined by the BMPA Directors.

C. CHANGES TO BMPA PROPERTIES

Directors of the BMPA are charged with maintaining and improving the properties of the *Field Cabin* and *Rocky Ledge* to make them safer and more livable for all. In general, the BMPA policy is to reach consensus on the changes made to the properties, and to value tradition and family history, bearing in mind that these properties are filled with memories and emotions for all.

In all cases, it is essential to communicate to inform all stakeholders of proposed changes before making improvements to the properties, unless such changes have been approved in a prior meeting of the BMPA. When changes require immediate attention, the BMPA seeks ways to streamline processes while maintaining the order and completeness of communication.

In general, major decisions are made thoughtfully and deliberatively taking into consideration reasons to leave things as they are even as we seek to improve and valuing the input of each member of the Association and committees.

ARTICLE VIII: CHANGES TO THIS DOCUMENT
Except for Article IX regarding dissolution, this document may be changed by agreement of at least 3/4 of the Directors.

ARTICLE IX: DISSOLUTION OF BLACHLY MAINE PROPERTIES ASSOCIATION, INC.
Should at any time it be the unanimous will of the current Directors in good standing to dissolve the BMPA, the assets of the BMPA shall be distributed as follows:
  i. All of the BMPA's outstanding debts shall first be paid.
  ii. Any remaining proceeds shall be distributed to one or more 501(c)3 public charities or educational institutions as agreed by the Directors.

* Article IX is irrevocable and may not be changed.

Author's Bio

Peter Macdonald Blachly is fond of saying he grew up on an island in Maine, though he spent the school year in Washington, DC. Peter is a restless soul whose lifetime of adventures and wide range of creative expression have included careers and avocations as a rock musician, yoga instructor, watercolor artist, trauma recovery coach, builder, sailor, teacher, mechanic, real estate developer, non-profit executive, licensed sea captain, and author. More can be read about these pursuits at www.petermacdonaldblachly.com.

Peter is glad to hear from readers, and can be contacted at petermacdonaldblachly@gmail.com

www.ingramcontent.com/pod-product-compliance
Lightning Source LLC
Chambersburg PA
CBHW042320090526
44585CB00024BA/2674